MARCHING
TO THE
DRUMS

MARCHING
TO THE
DRUMS

A HISTORY OF MILITARY
DRUMS AND DRUMMERS

JOHN NORRIS

To my grand-daughter, Harriett Eleanor May, whose attempts at playing the drum made amusing diversions during the time spent writing this book.

First published 2012

by Spellmount, an imprint of
The History Press
The Mill, Brimscombe Port
Stroud, Gloucestershire, GL5 2QG
www.thehistorypress.co.uk

© John Norris, 2012

The right of John Norris to be identified as the Author
of this work has been asserted in accordance with the
Copyrights, Designs and Patents Act 1988.

British Library Cataloguing in Publication Data.
A catalogue record for this book is available from the British Library.

ISBN 978 0 7524 6879 2

Typesetting and origination by The History Press
Manufacturing Managed by Jellyfish Print Solutions Ltd.
Printed in Malta.

CONTENTS

ACKNOWLEDGEMENTS

Firstly I would like to express my gratitude to my wife Elizabeth, who waits patiently and takes notes while I take photographs and talk at length. My thanks go to the many re-enactment groups who have spared the time to speak to me on subjects relating to the use of the drum across the ages and also for allowing me to photograph them for this work. I thank the event organisers where the re-enactments displays are staged, particularly Gary Howard who arranges Military Odyssey. I am also grateful to the staff of regimental museums who have given their time so freely. I would like to thank Jesper Ericsson of the Gordon Highlanders Regimental Museum in Scotland for the images and some background detail on the return of the drums to the regiment. I am most grateful to Michael Cornwall at the Wardrobe Museum in Salisbury for allowing photography and giving me personal explanations of artefacts. My special thanks go to Dave Sands of the Worcestershire Regimental Museum for his support in providing additional material on the black drummers of the 29th Regiment of Foot and for providing illustrations used in the work; Dr Geoffrey Dexter with whom I discussed the use of human skin as drum skins and gave me an idea for the opinion I reached, and Barabara Birley, assistant curator at the Vindolanda Trust at Hexham, for answering the difficult question about Roman army drummers. My thanks go to Captain R.W.C. Matthews, Assistant Regimental Adjutant of the Coldstream Guards, for his time in answering my questions concerning drummer boys. I thank English Heritage and their staff at the sites in their care for making my visits very rewarding. Finally I would like to thank Grahame Gillmore for providing some excellent images, Chris Harmon who talked at length about drummers across the centuries, and the rest of the Diehards who portray the Victorian army with such high levels of authenticity.

INTRODUCTION

As a young boy growing up on Jersey in the Channel Islands during the 1960s, I did many of the same things as some of my school friends, including joining the local Sea Cadet Corps. This organisation offered energetic lads the opportunity to go camping and sailing along with a range of other activities. There was also the corps of drums and as a member of this section of the organisation there came further opportunities such as travelling to England to participate in competitions with other units of Sea Cadets. We probably thought we were good and our long-suffering instructors, despite our undoubted awfulness, nevertheless encouraged us in our endeavours to produce a recognisable tune. Some lads played the bugle and for my part I tried the side drum. I remember thinking how heavy the thing was and how its large awkward size and shape made it unwieldy. Trying to march with the great weight slung over one's shoulder, banging against the left leg, was virtually impossible and I soon asked to go on the cymbals because not only were they easier to play but they were also more manageable, being lighter and smaller.

Over forty years later, reflecting back on those boyhood days it seems incredible to think that there was a time when lads at the age we were in the Sea Cadet Corps had served as drummers in armies and marched into battle while beating out a rhythm to encourage the fighting men. It must have been a terrifying prospect going into battle unarmed and yet these young boys did not flinch. The names of most have long since been forgotten, or were never properly recorded, such as the little French drummer boy trapped inside the slaughterhouse that was Hougoumont Farm during the Battle of Waterloo in June 1815. However, some are still remembered, such as André Estienne from Cadenet, France, who was decorated by Napoleon and has numerous statues around France, and there is a handful known from the bloody episode of the American Civil War. As an historian such incidents involving individuals hold more fascination than they would for the passing curiosity of a tourist.

On coming to England after completing my education I joined the Grenadier Guards and once more found myself marching to the beat of drums. This time,

er, it was as an infantryman taking part in ceremonies such as Trooping
..our on Horse Guards Parade in London rather than as a musician. Such
parades may seem like so much pomp and ceremony, but such pageantry served
a purpose and is part of regimental history. Delving into the role of drums and
drummers in military history, one comes to see them in a new and different
light. These were brave boys and men who stood shoulder to shoulder with
riflemen in battles all across Europe, North America, Africa and Russia. They
had to pace out to set an example so that the army would advance and the
casualty rate among drummers was extremely high. Even so, they did not flinch
and continued about their duties regardless.

The drum is universally regarded as being the most basic of all musical instruments and its use can be traced across the continents from the earliest times and
continues today with ceremonial occasions. Thousands of years ago the only
way of communicating on the battlefield was by means of visual or verbal commands. Visual signals could be negated by bad weather or the line of sight being
interrupted by obstacles such as woods or hills. Verbal commands were only
useful for communicating at close quarters and could become ineffective over
distance or drowned out by the noise of battle. Over time drums came to be
used to relay signals and distinctive commands could be passed on by the echoing thumps on the drum. Brass instruments such as the bugle would eventually
come to serve the same purpose as the drum, but that, as they say, is another
chapter in military history altogether.

Over the centuries, drums have evolved to become symbols of inspiration,
high morale and to signal victory. They have often been used to rally troops for
one final effort rather than giving up. The Hussite leader Jan Ziska, 1378–1424,
who campaigned in what is modern-day Bohemia and the Czech Republic,
is understood to have ordered that his skin be used to cover the drums so that
he may continue to lead his troops in battle after his death. Drums have also
been used to signal the shame of an individual being thrown out of the army
for actions which do not warrant imprisonment, but the perpetrator still had
to be seen to be punished for the sake of discipline. Some drums have passed
into legend, such as that taken by Sir Francis Drake on his voyages and which
is believed to sound when England needs the assistance of the man who helped
defeat the Spanish Armada in 1588.

Among the earliest militaristic societies to use the drum were the ancient
Egyptians, who left reliefs carved in stone to depict campaigns in the region of
the Sudan and Ethiopia showing drums deployed among the fighting men. For
all its militarism the Roman army did not widely use drums, but relied instead
on a range of other instruments including horns. It was not until the twelfth
century that Europeans were once more exposed to drums when they encountered kettledrums used to relay signals among the ranks of the Saracen armies
during the Crusades. Even the Janissaries (taken from the Turkish word *yeniceri*

to mean new troops) as mercenaries in the Turkish armies made extensive use of drums for marching, morale, signalling and to intimidate their enemies.

The Janissary band was called the *mehter* and its commander was known by the title of *Corbacibasi*, who was dressed most resplendently, as befitted his rank, in fine attire which included brilliant red robes and a large white turban decorated with peacock feathers. This Turkish formation had a reputation for producing very loud music with trumpets and drums, some of which, the kettledrums in particular, were noted for their enormous size. Such formations accompanied the Turkish army on campaigns, including the war against Hungary in 1526 and in particular the Siege of Vienna in 1529 where it was said that 400 drums were pounding constantly. This would have been an early example of what we today call psychological warfare, designed to undermine morale and weaken resistance. One hundred years earlier, drums had been used at the conclusion of a prolonged siege when Jeanne d'Arc (Joan of Arc) made a triumphal entry into the French city of Orleans to the sound of trumpets and drums. She, in turn, was only continuing an example set by King Edward III of England who had entered the French city of Calais after the siege in 1347. Apparently Edward had used drums at the Battle of Halidon Hill, where he decisively defeated the Scots in 1333, and thirteen years later at the Battle of Crécy on 26 August 1346 drums were used in battle as the troops moved about the battlefield. The French-born chronicler Jean Froissart (known as John Froissart in English), 1337–1405, recorded in his works that at the Battle of Crécy the Genoese crossbowmen serving as mercenaries in the French army moved to take up their positions to engage the English army to the beat of drums. Turkish drums had long enjoyed great renown and it was the Swiss mercenaries of the time who spread their influence, the instruments referred to around 1471 as *tambour des Perses* (Drums of Persia) and included kettledrums.

Drums were also a distinguishing feature among the forces of the region referred to as the Middle East, continuing through the Ottoman Empire of Turkey and indeed becoming known as 'Turkish Music' when it was adopted by western armies in the sixteenth century. As tactics developed and armies increased in size, the role of the drum to beat out a rhythm to which troops could march as a single unit was established, and the drummer took on a new level of importance on the battlefield.

First used among the infantry units and then the cavalry regiments who adopted the kettledrum mounted on special harnesses fitted to its horses, these drums could be used to relay various signals. Drummers would be deployed to raise the alarm in the event of a sudden attack against a camp and rouse the troops to its defence, signal the order to attack or to retreat, and even call for an armistice to discuss terms to end the fighting. As the construction of drums became more advanced in design, so an increased range of notes could be beaten and the drum became incorporated into bands which included flutes, bugles and horns, leading to martial music which is recognised the world over as being the sound to which soldiers march whilst on parade.

Today, whenever a military band marches through a town, the sound of the drums beating invariably draws in people to watch the parade. It seems that some men never stop being boys and even veterans proudly stand as the band passes by.

In Britain the term 'Drum' is often to be found used either as part of or the whole name of public houses across the country and these can be found in towns such as Leyton in London and Doncaster in South Yorkshire. Drums and drummers have been immortalised in poem, song and story. Rudyard Kipling uses the theme of drums and drummers in the British army in several of his works, for example the two heroes in his short story *The Drums of the Fore and Aft* are young drummer boys. In his poem 'Tommy', Kipling's words tell how the sound of drums can change peoples' attitude towards the military when he writes:

> Then it's Tommy this, an' Tommy that, an' Tommy ow's yer soul?
> But it's 'Thin red line of 'eroes' when the drums begin to roll,
> The drums begin to roll, my boys, the drums begin to roll,
> O it's 'Thin red line of 'eroes', when the drums begin to roll.

There are many fine regiments in the British army which have an association with drums other than those used by drummers of the regiment. For example, the 2/34th Regiment of Foot (Later known as the Border Regiment) captured drums from the French 34th Infantry Regiment at the Battle of Arroyo dos Molinos on 28 October 1811 during the fighting of the Peninsular campaign. These were made regimental trophies and for its part in the battle the regiment was given the engagement as a battle honour, since which time the regiment has commemorated Arroyo Day with the captured drums proudly paraded as a reminder of the event.

Radios, telephones and computers may have replaced the drum as the means of signalling on the battlefield, but the history and tradition of the drum still remains part of the military culture, with beating retreat, drumhead tattoos, Trooping the Colour and a host of other parades. However, not all military parades involving drummers were convened for the purposes of military reviews. Drummers were used to administer punishment to those defaulters sentenced to flogging; a drummer would beat out the count of the lashes and a drum-major usually oversaw the punishment. At sea the Royal Marines would beat to quarters and on land drummers were to be found serving on campaign. All this was unknown to me as a young Sea Cadet such a long time ago, but now the time has come to tell the story of the drum and the drummer in war.

ECHOES FROM THE PAST

The battle had entered its third day and the troops on both sides were exhausted. All attempts by the French to cross the Alpone River at Arcola in Italy had been repulsed by strong Austrian resistance. The battle had started on 15 November 1796 and early assaults by the French to cross the wooden bridge spanning the river had been forced back with heavy losses. On the second day of the fighting the commander of the French forces in Italy, a young energetic general by the name of Napoleon Bonaparte, personally led one of the attacks across the bridge with flag in hand. This spirited attempt to force a passage was also repulsed, and it seemed as though an impasse had been reached. The Austrians' superior firepower, including canister and grapeshot fired at close range from the artillery, was tearing into the ranks and inflicting a high rate of casualties on the French. The action had already cost the lives of nine generals and the French were facing defeat. Then on 17 November the seemingly impossible happened and some French troops managed to cross by swimming the freezing cold, swirling waters of the river with their weapons and equipment.

One of those crossing the river was a 19-year-old drummer boy by the name of André Estienne from the small town of Cadenet in the Luberon. He had managed to keep his drum dry by swimming with it perched on his head '…like an African native, carrying water in a pitcher…' Having crossed over with infantrymen, André adjusted his equipment, gathered himself together and, according to the story, he began to beat his drum with such vigour and force that the Austrians believed they had been taken by surprise and were surrounded. Taking advantage of the diversion which distracted the attention of the Austrian forces, the French main force stormed the bridge and captured the town of Arcola (sometimes written as Arcole). The battle was won and the Austrians were in retreat.

André Estienne had joined his regiment in the Luberon and was engaged in the Wars of the French Revolution and attached to the Army of Italy under Napoleon Bonaparte at Nice, who rewarded the young boy for his valour by presenting him with silver tokens. Today, in memory of his bravery, a statue of

André is to be seen in the square of his home town at Cadenet, where he is known as *La Tambour d'Arcole* (The Drummer of Arcole).

Some 4,500 years before young André exhibited his bravery in battle, the first military drums in history were entering service with the Egyptian army around 2,650BC, so beginning the story of the military drum which continues almost unbroken to this day. The country of Egypt falls into a region known as the Middle East, where over the centuries a number of military societies flourished, such as the Sumerians and the Parthians. Drums are among the oldest form of musical instrument and evidence of their existence goes back more than 8,000 years to around 6,000BC. Wall friezes and hieroglyphics dating from the period known as the Old Kingdom in Egypt, a timeline beginning from around 2,650BC to 2,152BC and encompassing the third to the sixth dynasties, have been discovered, although there are some authorities which also include the seventh dynasty, extending the timescale to 2,000BC.

In ancient Egyptian society, musical instruments were held in high regard and were of such importance that they are found in many paintings which decorate the interior of pyramids, often depicting deities such as Hather, Isis and Sekhmet engaged in playing a range of stringed instruments and even drums. These paintings are not just for decorative purposes; they tell a story which gives an insight into what was happening at that time. Through these images we can tell that drums were used in ancient Egypt and that the Pharaohs' armies almost certainly used them on the march during campaigns into the Sudan and Ethiopia. Musical instruments were also an integral part of Egyptian religious services and images mainly show women engaged in playing these and possibly even creating a rhythm. There were several main types of instruments in ancient Egypt, all hand held, including items known as *sistrums*, types of rattles made from metal, *crotals*, which were made from wood and 'slapped' together, trumpets and, of course, drums, which fell into two forms.

The first of these forms was the barrel-shaped drum, which was probably used exclusively by the military units of the army. These players would have been experienced musicians and most images show these drums being played with bare hands thumping out the beat. Military musicians had to audition for the role of drummer to prove their capability and there is a record of one drummer proving his talent by performing 7,000 'lengths' on a barrel-shaped drum. However, the account does not describe what actually constituted a 'length', but it is assumed to mean a rhythmical phrase to define drumming methods. No images have yet been discovered showing these drums being played using sticks, unlike for the round frame drum. The historian Lisa Manniche supports the theory that barrel-shaped drums were played by thumping with the hand because of the images showing them being played in such a fashion and because, as stated, no images showing them being struck using sticks have yet been found.

The round frame drum was also used in ancient Egypt and it is believed to have been developed around 1,400BC. Some examples have been found among grave goods at excavations during archaeological digs, along with painted and carved images which provide a picture to suggest these drums were played by female priestesses during religious ceremonies and other temple rituals. A drum was unearthed during excavations at Thebes in 1823 and this measured 18 inches (in) in height, with a diameter of 24in and was probably played using two sticks. In the book *When the Drummers Were Women*, the author Layne Redmond expands on this and, indeed, many images of the time do show women engaged in the act of drumming. Round frame drums are also understood to have sometimes been played aboard boats on the River Nile where they were used to set the timing for the oarsmen to row in unison. From this usage it was only a question of time before music, and drums in particular, particularly those bass-drum designs which have indefinite pitch, gradually came to find a wider role within the military and eventually onto the battlefield.

Drums are to be found in all societies across the continents of the world and come in all shapes and sizes. Drums are also one of the few musical instruments to be used for the specific martial purpose of signalling between military units on the battlefield and conveying a commander's orders to whole armies, such as advance and withdraw. A Chinese military adviser around 500BC suggested that the drum be given 'to the bold', presumably because they would stand firm in battle. This was certainly the belief of Sun Tzu, the Chinese officer, philosopher and author of *The Art of War* in the fifth century BC. Sun Tzu is sometimes known as Sun Wu or Sun Zi depending on the pronunciation and his most important and influential work is also known as *Bingfa*. In this important treatise he states that: 'Gongs and drums, banners and flags are employed to focus the attention of troops. When soldiers are united by signals, the bravest cannot advance alone, nor can the cowardly withdraw. This is the art of handling an army.' This is perhaps the earliest recognition of the importance of the use of drums and flags on the battlefield for relaying signals, and recognises how flags can be used as rallying points for troops when reforming on the battlefield. Sun Tzu is also informing us that even in these early times troops had a loyalty to regimental symbols, either drums or regimental flags, and would not abandon them either by advancing without them or withdrawing and leaving them behind. In this work, not only do we see many strategic and tactical recommendations, but also the beginning of regimental customs which armies around the world would adopt over the centuries.

The Chinese military used a form of drum called the *taigu*, which was used to set the marching pace and also for signalling on the battlefield. An account of an un-named battle by an anonymous warrior from around this time tells how drums were beaten with sticks and signals were beaten out, which must have been fairly typical of how drums were used across the region before spreading further afield to influence other armies down to Korea and then into Japan.

Visual signals using hands and flags were an obvious and reliable means of communicating and of passing on orders to troops. This method of signalling can be traced back to around 3,000BC, but it did, however, require constant vigilance to watch for the next set of signal flags and in battle this is not always possible. Despite this drawback the armies of ancient Egypt used flags for signalling, as did the Roman legions with their *vexillum* standards, the Vikings with their raven banners, and the religious symbols and coats of arms of the Crusades.

The voice has a limited range and can easily become lost among the mêlée of screams and shouts during battle and so drums and horns or bugles were seen as a natural progression to relaying signals because their sound can be carried further. In large armies the drum worked well as a signalling device, but it has been opined that as armies grew larger it became more difficult to relay signals using drums. This may have been correct in some cases where the mass was not working as a truly cohesive unit. In the case of the Mongols where a *tuman*, or army of 10,000 and up to 100,000 men, worked as a co-ordinated force, the drum was successfully used to pass on signals. Admittedly, it helped greatly that the Mongols communicated their commander's intentions down to the smallest group prior to engaging the enemy so that each man was aware of what he had to do. Even in later centuries when armies began to use gunpowder weapons, the drum was found to still have a place on the battlefield and drummers were present at Waterloo, the Crimean War and throughout the American Civil War, which were all fought at different periods in the nineteenth century.

All drums comprise an outer body or 'shell' formed into an open-ended tube, over which is stretched an animal skin which has been treated and prepared specially for use on the drum. The traditional material used for drumheads was always animal skin, usually calf's leather, but today some plastics are used. There is a drawback to the use of natural animal skin, which is that rain or any other form of dampness can cause it to become slack, thereby affecting its sound, and so it has to be capable of being tightened. Conversely, if the skin becomes too dry it will split and the drum will be equally useless. The calfskin had to be prepared in a special process involving several stages of preparation to make it useful for drum coverings.

The method of preserving leather so that it does not decompose and can be used to make drum skins, belts, boots, gloves and other equipment, is called tanning. The process was known in South Asia perhaps as early as 7,000BC and the process spread so that by 2,500BC it was known to the Sumerians and the Egyptians. Ancient armies used leather for a variety of purposes, including the manufacture of armour and helmets for head protection, and the elastic properties leather possesses meant it made an excellent covering for drumheads.

The tanning process involved cleaning the skins and soaking them in special agents of tannin compounds in water to break down the natural protein structure so that it was no longer raw or untreated hide. It was a time-consuming process and many hundreds of people would have been employed in processing leather. Over time the demand for leather increased as harnesses and saddles for horses were required, and, as armies increased in size, so more leather was required for more equipment. This included skins for drums as more drummers had to be deployed with the larger armies if signalling was to be maintained.

Preparing leather was also an extremely pungent process, which at one time involved a vast quantity of human urine along with other noxious substances such as arsenic sulphide to remove the hair from the hides. It was a toxic mix and could produce madness, blindness or even both among those in the leather-working trade. Despite its obvious importance to the military societies, the production of leather was seen as a very demeaning task. Indeed, in some societies handling leather and human urine was completed by only the lowest of social castes. In 1047 a young 21-year-old Norman duke by the name of William besieged the castle at Alençon, lying on the Orne River in Lower Normandy, France. He was taunted in his efforts by the defenders who draped leather hides over the walls to remind the illegitimate duke that his mother had been a lowly tanner of leather. He was far from amused by the gesture and when he captured the site he ordered the mutilation of the thirty-two defenders by having their hands and feet chopped off and then thrown over the walls. The young duke is perhaps better known as William the Conqueror, who later defeated the English army of Harold at the Battle of Hastings in 1066.

The drum shell itself can be made from wood or metal and whilst pottery shells for drums do exist, the fragility of the material precludes it from being employed in military use where it would most likely break during the violent activity on a battlefield. Examples of drums made entirely of cast bronze have been discovered in China and these have been dated back to the Shang Dynasty of around 1,600 to 1,100BC. Archaeologists working at a location in East China have also recently excavated shards of porcelain at the site of a celadon pottery workshop dated to around 618 to 907AD during the Tang Dynasty in the region of Yugan County in the Jiangxi Province. These fragments have been pieced together and identified as the remains of porcelain waist drums, with a body length measuring some 16in and a diameter of 8in. The style is believed to have been popular and may have even influenced the design of drums in other regions. However, due to the fragile nature of their construction these drums must be ruled out as being intended for military use on the battlefield where the rigours would have led to them becoming damaged or broken. It must therefore be concluded that such drums were intended purely for either ceremonial or parade use, possibly to celebrate military victories. Pottery drum shells from an earlier period have also been discovered at an archaeological excavation at a site near Taosi, close to the Yellow River. These have been dated to around 2,000BC, possibly during the Zia Dynasty, and some show signs of having been decorated with red colouring which traditionally was used as a symbol of a ruler's power. Some Chinese drums were made in one piece using a hollowed-out tree trunk and some of these may have measured as much as 3ft in height and may have been the types used by the military. The German writer J. Schreyer noted as early as 1681 how some tribes in Africa: '… take a [clay] pot and bind a skin over it, and on this pot the women beat with their hands and fingers for these are their drums (*trummeln*) and kettledrums (*paucken*)'. This is an example of how different cultures, despite being separated by thousands of miles, evolved along similar lines and here in this scene the observer is recording women beating drums as in the Egyptian society of some 3,000 years earlier and also using pottery shells in the same way which we now know were used to form drums in China. In the Middle East similar clay drum shells have been discovered and it is believed these may have been covered with a drum skin of either donkey or goat stretched over the end. Some examples of wooden drum shells have also been found and these would have been covered in animal skins for the drumheads.

One of the earliest types of drum is that form known as 'frame', which has a body or shell with a shallow depth and has a diameter greater than its depth. It is a very old form of design, the drum skin being attached firmly to the wooden shell, which prevents the tension from being adjusted to alter the pitch. The circular shape of the shell is formed by a single piece of wood bent round, with the two ends joined together using a scarf joint cut at a very sharp angle to allow the ends to be fixed together using glue or nails. Examples have been discovered in various cultures from Europe to Asia and accorded different terms such as *daffu* or *kanjira* in India, *bodran* in Ireland and *daf* in some Middle Eastern countries. In Brazil it is called the *tamborim* and in Europe, where metal discs are attached to the frame, it is known as the tambourine. This evolved differently from the drum used by the military, and frame drums were more likely to be used for parades or festivals as opposed to being used for signalling on the battlefield.

At first it may have been that the banging of a drum was used to attract the attention of the troops, or at least unit commanders, and cause them to look at the flags which were the more traditional means of signalling on the battlefield. Over time, forms of communication combined with flags and drums were placed together in some military societies, later to be joined by trumpets. This combination of drums and flags to relay orders continued into the nineteenth century and each developed its own unique set of patterns for orders. Flags developed into a method known as semaphore signalling and drums developed 'rolls' as signals. It was a method which worked extremely well and control could be exercised over single, small units or larger formations with a number of drummers being dispersed through the army.

IN THE BEGINNING

The Roman military society, for all its innovations and quickness to grasp the importance of advances, was one of those few establishments which did not make use of drums and preferred instead to rely on wind instruments such as the tuba or *cornu*. The Roman philosopher Boethius believed '… music is part of us, and either ennobles or degrades our behaviour'. The poet Juvenal thought that '… of all the noises, I think music is the least disagreeable'. The Romans would almost certainly have been familiar with drums through contact with Egyptian religious ceremonies and with its military. Because of this, it has been opined that some units of the Roman army may have been inspired to use drums in an unofficial capacity. However, despite this theory the Roman army never used drums either to signal or as an aid to keeping step on the march. Staff at the ongoing archaeological excavation at the Roman frontier fort of Vindolanda in Northumberland confirm that they have never uncovered any positive evidence to show the Roman army used drums. A number of other highly respected research groups on Roman military equipment, including the world-famous Ermine Street Guard, also confirm that there is no evidence to support the suggestion that the Roman army ever used drums. The Romans were not alone in this negative opinion of drums and most of the earlier Greek City States did not use drums either, but rather opted for the more gentle sound of flutes to accompany their troops when going into battle. When the Roman Empire began to contract and leave Europe in the early fifth century AD, it left behind a vacuum which was filled by various local tribal leaders, some more warlike than others, along with a wealth of technology and other skills. Some of these Roman influences fell into disuse over time while others were maintained, such as styles of weaponry, but as drums had never been a part of the Roman army they were not found in post-Roman Europe.

The drum is one of the most basic designs of all musical instruments and because of its simplicity it was easy for different cultures to replicate examples they had come into contact with and develop their own style. The drum by its very nature is tubular in construction and varies in depth to control its resonance when being beaten by hand or struck with a stick. Some drum designs, such as those from India and China, have a barrel-like shape while some are goblet-shaped, which usually tend to only have one membrane covering and generally originate from the Middle East and are known as *durabuka*. The wooden shell of a drum is not overly complicated to produce and so is common even among primitive societies. Attaching the membrane to the shell using small nails, pegs, glue or even a binding would not be beyond the capability of such societies which would have been using similar techniques to attach spearheads to wooden shafts for the purpose of hunting or for warfare in the more militaristic groups. Some drum designs were developed with twine attached to the membranes, referred to as the 'lacing', and is common on double-headed drums and used as a means of allowing more tension to be exerted on the membranes to adjust the sound. This lacing could take the form known as 'W' or 'Y' style from the pattern it formed. Throughout the centuries, drums have been used in many rituals, from religious ceremonies to royal precessions. In Africa, for example, drums have been used to fulfil duties in both roles. In Europe the drum was absent for many years until it was gradually re-introduced over time, becoming increasingly widespread during the sixteenth and seventeenth centuries. Sometimes being called *tabour* or *timpani*, these drums were reserved for special occasions and used mainly in rituals involving pageantry of royalty.

The drum, very early on in its development, came to be used as a form of communicating messages over considerable distances using a range of coded signals. All drums, including the Indian *bayan* and the Japanese *tsuzumi*, are classified as membranophones, which is to say the sound they emit is created when the membrane covering of the shell is struck either by hand or with a stick so as to cause it to vibrate. It is a simple yet effective means of creating distinctive sound patterns and evidence of drums can be found all over the world. The Japanese historical chronicle *Gunji Yoshu* records how the form of a drum known as a *taiko* was used to beat out signals to summon allies to battle and how the *taiko yaku* (drummer) set the pace of marching, usually around six paces to the beat. The *taiko* drum is believed to have originated in China some time during the Yayoi period (500BC to 300AD) where it also had a martial use as a signalling device on the battlefield. Today, *taiko* drums are used during special ceremonies and have even developed into an art form for public entertainment with performances being given at concerts. Drummers in ancient India, for example, used a range of strokes of the hand to beat a rhythm using a drum such as the *tabla*. Other drums in use in India included the *dholak*, which could be tuned by adjusting the tension of the strings attaching the skin to the body, usually by means of a wooden peg, and this either slackened off or tightened the skin to alter the pitch. The *bayan* or *doogi* was another drum developed in India and this was similar in style to a drum used in Egypt, being played in a like fashion, using only the hands. A range of other types of drum were developed and used in India including the *dhol*, *chenda* and *dhimay*.

In seventh-century India, Hindu armies used drums to rouse the troops from their sleep and a range of signals also alerted them to the distance they had to march that day. The author of the *Kalingattu Parani* (a poem about the victory of the Chola King in around 1,000BC) records how a Hindu army on the march was most impressive with: '… conch-shells sounded, the big drums thundered, and the reeds and pipes squeaked till the ears of the elephants… were deafened…' There are many Indian records containing accounts of battles which tell how drums were used to inspire the troops whilst trying to unsettle the enemy. In Thailand, drums were beaten to herald the approach of victorious armies, often led in procession by war elephants. To train elephants for warfare they were subjected to the sound of drums being beaten to make them used to such noises on the battlefield. Indian armies also used camels to carry drums for use on the battlefield and there are some illustrations which show them being used in such a role.

In South America, excavations of archaeological sites have revealed evidence of the use of drums in Aztec, Mayan and Incan cultures, which were particularly militaristic societies. Carvings in stone reliefs show drums being used by these civilisations, but to what extent and whether they were used widely as forms of signalling on the battlefield is not yet entirely clear. Such evidence is important in understanding the use of drums within the society as a whole, in exactly the same way as the Egyptian tomb paintings discovered in the pyramids. It is known that the Aztec military in what is modern-day Mexico used a type of drum called the *tlalpanhuehuetl*. The drum was wooden and stood over 3ft in height, with the drumhead made of jaguar skin and decorated with images of birds and other animals. The Incas who lived in what is modern-day Peru and Chile are also known to have beat war drums when going into battle. Similarly, in the North American continent the Native American tribes also used drums for ceremonial purposes, to intimidate enemy tribes and as signals. These were crudely made but functional devices and when white European settlers colonised the lands these native tribes utilised discarded items such as wooden barrels, covering them with hides and fashioning them into extemporised drums.

It would appear that, for whatever reason, drums either fell out of use in the European military societies or had never been considered of any real relevance and therefore were not included in the structure of a military unit. Drums would almost certainly have been known about, but even in the eleventh century they do not appear as part of the European military system and there is no imagery of them in the Bayeaux Tapestry which records in considerable detail the Norman Conquest of Britain in 1066. It would not be until the Crusades were undertaken, which were a series of religious expeditionary wars conducted between 1096 and 1291, that the European armies found themselves exposed to the effects of the drum, which was an important object in the structure of the Muslim military forces. This is an opinion supported by the historian David Nicolle, who writes that: 'The increasing importance of military drums similarly almost certainly reflected Islamic musical influence via the Crusades, Sicily and Spain.' As a result, a number of other instruments were introduced into European culture and the drums in particular had their names treated to European translations, so that the *tablah* became the *tabor* and the *naqqarah* became the small *naker*.

We learn of Crusaders coming into contact with drums from the writings of leading figures such as Jean de Joinville, who fought at the Battle of Mansourah (sometimes written as Mansura) on 8 February 1250 during the Seventh Crusade (1248–1254). A force of French knights attempted to capture the town, but upon entering it the Muslim forces proceeded to cut them to pieces. Jean de Joinville, who was badly wounded in the fight, later wrote: 'As I stood there on foot with my knights, wounded as I have told you, King Louis came up at the head of his battalions, with a great sound of shouting, trumpets and kettledrums'. The attack continued and de Joinville wrote of the battle's progress how: 'As the [French] royal army began to move there was once again a great sound of trumpets, kettledrums and Saracen horns'. From this eyewitness account it would appear that drums were beginning to enter into use with European Crusader forces by the early to middle period of the thirteenth century. The European Crusaders, as we see here, used trumpets and adopted drums to use for signalling purposes, even using them to signal between vessels sailing in convoy. The order of the Knights Templar from this period are also known to have used bells to awaken the soldiers and to sound the alarm in the event of them being attacked. These would not have been small, delicate devices but rather large, clanging versions which would have echoed around the walls of a building, leaving no-one in any doubt that an alarm was being rung.

The term we use today to describe the area of the Middle East is a relatively modern expression and encompasses the region lying between longitude 24° and 60° east, taking in Asiatic Turkey, Iraq, Iran and several other states in the area. Over the centuries, many military societies came to flourish in this region and many great campaigns were fought here, including Megiddo, which is one of the earliest recorded battles from around 1,468BC. One of the most prominent military societies from the mid-thirteenth century was the Mamelukes; professional Islamic soldiers, usually of slave origins, who placed great value on bands of musicians. At one point the sultan is known to have had forty-four drums, four *hautbois* (oboes) and twenty trumpets grouped as a band. It was considered a great honour to be allowed to have a band and those amirs who were granted permission were given the title of 'Lords of the Drums'. It is believed that about thirty such amirs were to be given the honour of having a band and each would have had command of forty horsemen, with a band of ten drums, two *hautbois* and four trumpets. To be granted permission for a band was an elite status symbol for amirs, who would usually serve as Islamic officers, whilst others may have held office as frontier governors. The drums in such cases were more than just a statement of rank as they had a specific role in battle, being used to undermine an enemy's confidence and hopefully cause chaos in the ranks of an opposing army, particularly among the horses which would have been unaccustomed to such sustained noise. The Muslim horses on the other hand would have been quite used to the sound of the drums, probably being introduced to the rhythmic pounding as part of the training for warfare.

The noise produced by a drum is a short but continuous sound, which can be achieved by striking the drumhead rapidly. The side drum creates a very short sound and cannot be beaten fast enough to produce what seems like a continuous sound, and so the distinctive 'rat-a-tat-tat' is produced. With the bass drum the drummer can strike alternatively to produce the effect of a continuous sound. The rhythm to achieve this effect has to be practised because if struck too quickly the drummer's action will negate the effect of the vibration of the preceding stroke. The same principle applies to kettledrums or *nakers* carried in pairs, as the drummer could strike these alternatively to give what seemed like a continuous sound. Such an unending noise would have been alien to the ears of the European Crusaders to whom the loudest sound they may have ever previously heard would have been either a thunderclap or the ringing of a bell, both of which are of relatively short duration. Therefore, a continuous rumble of many drums would have been terrifying and psychologically disturbing to the men and horses exposed to it for the first time.

Whilst drums, especially the bowl-shaped type known as *nakers* or kettledrums, would continue to be featured in the Saracen battle line, its influence was slow to spread to European armies. Indeed, it was not until sometime in the sixteenth century that drums really began to be incorporated into European armies, where it was referred to as 'Turkish music' from the fact that Ottoman Turkish forces used drums extensively. Evidence for this is shown in paintings dating to around 1540 and shows drummers and pipers in military dress. In the Muslim armies, drum signals were used as a means to summon the soldiers to assemble for inspection and also to receive their pay. This was also practiced in the Persian army from around the eighth century AD onwards, when a pair of drums signalled the Saffarid troops for the annual review usually around the time of a festival known as Nawruz at the beginning of the New Year. The side drum and possibly the kettledrum are also widely believed to have been introduced by Swiss and Germanic mercenaries probably around the late fourteenth century, first either into Spain or France and then spreading to other European countries.

Battle tactics developed by the Byzantine armies of the eastern Mediterranean area as early as the fifth century AD called for the drum master in any enemy Turkish force to be identified and singled out so that he might either be killed or captured in order that the means of communicating using drum signals may be disrupted or destroyed. (It is interesting to note that by comparison at this time, Europe was entering a period known as the 'Dark Ages' because positive recorded history is very scant.) This Byzantine strategy of capturing or killing the drum master of their traditional Turkish enemy had actually been devised relatively early and shown to be effective in disrupting the enemy's tactical formations on the battlefield. The identification of the drum master could be completed fairly quickly and easily because the commander of a Turkish army usually took station on the highest point of ground so that he could overlook the battlefield and study the progress of the engagement. Accompanying him in this position would have been a corps of drummers, who would pound out signals to the senior lieutenants of units in the field. Some 700 years later, in the thirteenth century, the Mameluke forces were using drums and trumpets in the same manner to pass signals to tactical formations, including the signals to re-assemble in readiness to prepare for a possible counter-attack. The Mameluke war drums, like other military societies, were often elaborately decorated with tassels of horsehair and other decorative designs, sometimes denoting the station or rank of the officer within the camp. This decoration is continued today with the drums of the regimental bands being emblazoned with the names of battle honours, regimental badges, crests and mottos.

Around the second half of the twelfth century, a disparate collective of tribes began to unify and form into an immensely powerful group known as the Mongols. The group was headed by a leader called Temujin (sometimes written as Temuchin), but who is best known to history as either Chingis Khan or Genghis Khan. By 1206 he had come to be regarded as head of all those tribes who lived in the vastnesses of the steppe region of central Asia, north of the Gobi Desert and south of the Siberian forests. From this scattered group of people Genghis Khan formed a vast army of mounted warriors, who from the very beginning of their offensive campaigns, first against China to be followed by others, swept all before them. Successive leaders, or Khans, such as Ogedei would maintain the Mongols' military dominance across the region and reassert the fear in the conquered peoples' minds that the Mongols were the 'Wrath of God', as it had been in the time of Genghis.

By the time of the leadership of Timur-i Lank, the grandson of Kublai Khan, who ruled over the Mongols from 1294 until 1307, the great days of the Mongol campaigns were over and they were becoming increasingly influenced by Turkish methods. But there were still some true aspects of Mongol militarism which persisted because it was tried and tested, and had proved successful in the past. For example, the structure of the army remained based on the decimal principle, with the smallest unit of ten men being commanded by a *bashi*. Other officers known as the *yaz bashi* commanded 100 men and a *ming bashi* officer commanded 1,000 men. The officer class was called Aymak, with the most senior being known as Amirs, some of whom had honorary titles such as *bahadur*, and these were identified by special standards, flags and drums, some of which were mounted on harnesses fitted to camels. These men led the armies, still known as *tumans*, which numbered up to 10,000 men. The sub-units of 1,000 men were called *bin liq* and those of 100 men were either called *goshun* or *yuzliq*. The campaign of 1303 led into Syria by Timur-i Link reached its climax when his army was defeated at the Battle of Marj-as-Suffar by a force of Mamelukes on 20 April. This event marked the beginning of the end for the Mongols as a credible unified force, and over the next eight decades the once-powerful Mongol Empire broke up into smaller groups. Some remained independent whilst others were defeated and absorbed into larger dominant societies, a process which was completed during the Chinese Ming Dynasty in 1386 at the Battle of Kerulen River. During a battle, the Chinese army used drums to signal an advance, but sounded large gongs to signal a retreat. The use of two such distinct sounds would have avoided confusion and the troops under command would have responded instinctively.

From the thirteenth century onwards, the Mamelukes, an Arabic term meaning slaves, began to ascend as the dominant military force in the Middle East region, especially in areas such as Egypt and Syria. This was sealed when they defeated the Mongol army at the Battle of Marj-as-Suffar in 1303. The Mamelukes may have had a history which evolved from humble slave origins, but over time they would come to develop their own tactics and strategies for attack, counter-attack and defence. During the ninth century AD, the Muslim rulers began to make increasing use of slaves in the military and these conscripted troops came mainly originated from the region of Turkey. They were trained primarily as mounted archers, equipped with lances and taught the skills written in the *furusiyya* manuals of the time. There may have been some resentment to being enslaved, but the Mamelukes learned how to make themselves indispensable to their Muslim masters and turned this to their advantage. The Mamelukes were also referred to as *ghulams* (pages) to denote their status as a servant who had often been acquired as a young man and raised in the homes of the masters they were to serve. Over time some learned a range of skills, including military theories, and by displaying loyalty to their Muslim masters gained their trust. This position was not abused at first and they remained staunchly loyal, which was rewarded by being granted their freedom. They continued to serve the Ayyubid caliph and, biding their time, some Mamelukes eventually gained more power and were promoted to positions which enabled them, by the time of the Seventh Crusade 1249–1250, to rise in revolt to overthrow Turanshah. The power of the Mamelukes became such that by 1260 they were able to seize the throne of Egypt. With this move they established a ruling Levantine dynasty which had risen from slave soldier status. It was a lineage that would last for over 250 years until finally they were defeated during the Ottoman Conquest which was conducted between 1488 and 1517. Even so, the Mamelukes would remain a military force to be reckoned with and could still exert influence. The early years of the Mameluke rule were not settled and there was intrigue, plotting and assassinations before the stable influence of the eminent Sultan Baybars (sometimes written as Baibars) began his dynasty. The first Mameluke Sultan Aidik had been murdered in 1250 by his wife Queen Shajar ud-Durr, the widow of the late al-Salih. She would in turn be murdered several years later by supporters of Aidik in a belated act of revenge. Kotuz then succeeded in 1257, but he too was murdered by his able lieutenant, Baybars, following their victory over the Mongols at the Battle of Ain Jalut in 1260. With stability now established in their ranks, the Mamelukes could grow in power and influence.

At the Battle of Ain Jalut on 3 September 1260, Kotuz (also known as Qutuz) led a Mameluke army of 12,000 to victory over the Mongol army led by Kitboga. Kotuz followed this up by regrouping at Cairo and gathering an army believed to have been some 120,000 strong. He pursued the Mongols and killed Kitboga in the process, which led to the Mongols, now commanded by Bereke, converting to Islam and entering into an alliance with Baybars and the Mamelukes. In April 1291 the Mamelukes, led by Khalil Malik al-Ashraf, seized the city of Acre using at least 100 special siege engines. The Crusaders lost their last major stronghold in the Kingdom of Jerusalem and were eventually forced out of the Holy Land, taking many influences with them, including the drum. In their wake the Mamelukes remained as the dominant force and established an economic and cultural ruling class that became pre-eminent in Egypt. It was a reign that would last for 500 years and would only truly come to an end when they were decisively beaten by a French army, commanded by Napoleon Bonaparte, at the Battle of the Pyramids on 21 July 1798. Even in defeat the Mamelukes still exerted an influence and the victorious French began to adopt a style of Egyptian dress and to carry Mameluke-style swords. Napoleon even acquired an Arab-bred horse in 1799 after the Battle of Aboukir on 25 July. He called the horse Marengo and he would ride the stallion in every campaign, including his ill-fated Russian operation in 1812 and his final battle at Waterloo against the Duke of Wellington on 18 June 1815. Indeed, he is shown in many paintings mounted on Marengo and sometimes shown accompanied by his manservant, a Mameluke by the name of Roustam Raza, who had been presented to Napoleon by a sheik from Cairo. The Mameluke effect would also spread to influence the British army in the region, which also adopted Mameluke-style swords for dress occasions. They also adopted Turkish instruments, sometimes called the 'Turkish Bells', 'Chinese Hat' or 'Jingling Johnnie', which was an elaborately decorated staff with bells and usually topped with a crescent shape. A painting by E. Hull dated 1829 shows a drummer of the Grenadier Guards complete with turban adorned with a crescent and plume, illustrating the further spread of Turkish influence. Both the drum and the 'Jingling Johnnie' were known to have been used by the Mamelukes to signal rallying calls during battle. Looking forward more than 100 years to the 1930s and the rise of the Nazi Party in Hitler's Germany, and the SS in particular, branches of the German armed forces used similar standards which were called *Schellenbaum* (Bell Tree). Even today some variations on this device can still be seen in modern military bands.

In the fourteenth century the Mameluke forces included cavalry in their structure, especially the continuance of mounted archers whose skills were used to great effect. Writing in the early fourteenth century, Ibn Khaldun has left a description of how Mameluke forces were usually arranged in ranks three deep. On coming into position on the battlefield the riders would dismount and remove arrows from the carry pouch or quiver and push them tip first into the ground where they were readily at hand for use. The dismounted archers then targeted the enemy drummers and shot flights of arrows at them in an attempt to kill them or force them to flee, thereby preventing signals from being relayed by drum beat. The Mamelukes in turn used drummers and flags to pass signals to troops across the battlefield and these were always well protected against attack. The dismounted archers in their serried triple ranks could advance or withdraw in an orderly manner, with at least two ranks shooting arrows to cover the movement of the third rank. They also devised a method of erecting a tower or some kind of elevated platform if the battlefield was flat, and from this point the commander could issue commands which in turn were relayed as signals in the form of drum beats.

Obviously the troops would have been conditioned to respond to the drum signals as they were beaten, and the identification of such signals would have been taught to all new troops during their basic training. However, not all new recruits would have been able to commit these to memory and it would have been through the experience of the older troops that the identification of these signals were reaffirmed to the younger, less experienced troops. Once learned, though, the troops, or at least their unit commander who would recognise such signals, would have responded instinctively to the signal and ordered the drill movement to be completed in unison.

The Mamelukes established a corps of drums known as the *tablkhanah* and it was given a status of great importance. The idea of such drum corps was taken up by the Ottoman Turks who incorporated the formation into their *mehterhane*, which was their military music department. This was a fine example of imitation being the sincerest form of flattery and although drums were used to communicate signals on the battlefield, other instruments such as trumpets could also be used as signalling devices. The military societies of the Mamelukes and the Turks were predominantly mounted and so it was only natural that special drums be developed for use with cavalry troops on horseback. For this reason a series of small drums fitted into leather frames which could then be attached to a saddle were developed and used by the Mamelukes of the late period. The Ottoman Turks took up the idea and continued to use it for the purpose of calling a re-assembly signal to troops who had become scattered after an action. Such drums were evidently the earliest form which would become the kettledrums in European armies at a later date.

The first Mameluke army tactics had been developed in the thirteenth century when they included cavalry charges directed against the centre of an enemy's forces where the signal flags and drummers were positioned, almost exactly in the same manner as the Byzantine forces of 600 years earlier. This was intentionally meant to kill these signallers in order to prevent messages being relayed through an army. The Mamelukes themselves relied on drums, trumpets and flags to control the movements of their own formations on the battlefield and knew the importance of protecting these devices at all costs. Once the signals had been relayed, the troops tended to complete their movements without any further accompaniment by drums or trumpets. They knew from experience that once they eliminated an enemy's methods of signalling, it would cause a severe disruption and even a breakdown of signals being passed on. The Mamelukes had learned many of their battlefield tactics from the Mongols, who also knew the importance of drums and flags for signalling.

In the sixth century AD the Byzantines believed that an overuse of trumpets on the battlefield could cause confusion as signalling devices. The Sassanians on the other hand made extensive use of trumpets to signal the commencement of battle, to maintain morale among the troops during battle and as a salute when senior commanders entered the military camp. Attitudes towards trumpets changed over the centuries so that by the tenth century the Byzantines had abandoned the idea that the movement of troops in silence was more impressive on the battlefield and followed Arab and Turkish trends to introduce military bands and the use of trumpets, horns, drums and cymbals. By the eleventh century the Byzantines were using drum signals to rouse the camp and flutes were also played when on the march. This practice would continue through the great wars of the nineteenth century and drummers and buglers also served on the ships of the line.

Even before the rise of the military societies the drum was widely spread as an instrument and used on all continents where tribal groups existed. This included the deep, impenetrable jungles of South America, across Asia and throughout the vastness of Africa. Indeed, the author Anthony Storr in his book *Music and the Mind* states that: 'No culture so far discovered lacks music. Making music appears to be one of the fundamental activities of mankind; as characteristically human as drawing and painting.' In fact, in North Africa some rulers used the drum as a symbol to denote their royal status. Among the tribes that inhabited the region, including the Berber tribes, drum groups were created. As early as the eleventh century these drummers were more than simply just musicians; they were an important part of the military infrastructures with a specific role on the battlefield and it has been estimated that the sound of these early drums could carry as far as 5 miles. Of course, in those days the world was a far quieter place and noises such as drum beats would have alerted those in the vicinity.

However, not everyone approved of drums and the early Muslim Murabit rulers governing a tribe of religious volunteers guarding the Muslim frontiers of North Africa disliked them because they believed drums were a reminder of African paganism. Despite this, the use of the drum continued and even spread gradually into other Muslim-held areas such as Andalusia in Spain and across the

Iberian Peninsular. It was in this region that drums began to be used to spread panic among the cavalry units of the Christian armies, whose horses had never experienced such a noise before. The pounding drums also unnerved some of the soldiers, while at the same time improving the morale among Muslim troops. The later Muwahhid expanded on this use of drums in what is surely an early example of psychological warfare designed to unsettle or cause discomfort among one's enemies. The Muwahhid ordered groups of drums to be massed together and they were mounted on special frames, elaborately decorated with green and gold furnishings. The noise of their beat as they were pounded in unison would have been astonishing to the ears of Christian troops, who not have heard anything like it before. In central Asia, a world away from Andalusia and North Africa, the Turco-Mongols refined the tradition of military music which they had established. The senior Khagan, or ruler, could have his own personal group of up to eighty musicians with horns, cymbals and drums. This group could also be mounted during time of battle to provide them with mobility and enable them to move about and signal troops to manoeuvre. Some of the older, more experienced drummers were used to beat loud signals on the largest drums, sounding the order to advance and for battle to commence.

Over the centuries the drum had come a long way to being firmly established as a military object in the same tradition as battle flags and standards, and was a far cry from its humble and primitive tribal origins. Some regiments viewed the loss of their drums in battle as a great disgrace and would go to great lengths to prevent their capture to avoid the shame it would bring. By the same token, to capture an enemy's drums, Regimental Colours or Regimental Standard, such as the 'Eagle' of the French army in the time of the Napoleonic Wars, was viewed as a great achievement. For example, the 3rd King's Own Hussars in the British army did not have their regimental battle honours embroidered on the kettle-drum banners draped around the drums they had captured from the French at the Battle of Dettingen in June 1743, and instead the regiment engraved them on the silver drums as a regimental trophy. On 28 October 1811, during the Peninsular War, the British 34th Regiment of Foot (later to become the Border Regiment), whilst serving as part of Sir Rowland Hill's division, found itself facing its opposite French number, the 34eme Regiment de Ligne, during an engagement at the village of Arroyo dos Molinos in Spain. During the fighting, Sergeant Moses Simpson of the British 34th Regiment of Foot fought a desperate hand-to-hand struggle with the French drum-major and succeeded in wrestling the mace from his grasp. This was indeed a trophy, but it was made all the more complete with the capture of most of the drums of the French 34eme Regiment. The drums are today paraded as regimental trophies on the 28 October each year to commemorate the action. Similarly, the trumpet major of the 5th Dragoon Guards (Princess Charlotte of Wales's) for many years carried a drum-major's mace or staff which had been captured from the French 66eme Regiment at the Battle of Salamanca in July 1812. Drums had now become elevated from rather humble origins to revered regimental symbols and part of history and tradition. In the collection held at Le Musée de l'Empéri in Provence in France, a drum captured from the 83rd Regiment of Foot (later to become the Royal Irish Rifles) is on display to balance out trophies displayed from the battlefield. Across the world drums are on display in military museums to commemorate battles fought and lost, but mainly those which were won.

THE SPREAD OF THE
MILITARY DRUM

Out of all the instruments in a martial band, it is perhaps the drum which stands out prominently due to its many variations. Large or small, this instrument conjures up evocations of past glories on battlefields from Blenheim and Waterloo to Inkerman and Gettysburg, where the drum was ever-present. Even on warships the drum was used to summon crews to hasten to their battle stations and carry out orders to the 'rat-a-tat-tat' as the drummer urgently beat out his signal. Regimental bands when parading through the streets attracted young and old alike with the beat of the drum. Recruiting parties in England during the eighteenth century often comprised an officer, two non-commissioned officers and a drummer. As armies across Europe continued to grow in size, so the demand for more recruits grew. In some countries recruits were raised by conscription and then marched off to their depots to the accompaniment of drums, but in England recruiting was done by 'Beat of the drum' where the sound of a drummer playing '… the points of war…' usually brought out the curious to see what all the fuss was about. Colonels of regiments were given 'beating orders' so that 'By Beat of Drum or otherwise to raise so many men as are found to be wanting.'

The recruiting party usually established itself in an inn or tavern where the unwary were plied with drink to lower their resistance to the persuasive talk of the recruiting officer and NCOs. Life-size wooden figures painted in uniforms were sometimes placed outside the tavern to encourage potential recruits to visit. Such tactics to get a man to enlist by fair means or foul did not suit all recruiting staff and in 1705 Captain Blackadder wrote of his mission: 'This vexing trade of recruiting depresses my mind. I am the unfittest for it of any man in the army, and have not the least talent for it in any way. Sobriety is here a bar to success. I see the greatest rakes are the best recruiters. I cannot ramble, and rove, and tell stories, and wheedle and insinuate, if my life were lying at stake'. In France, recruiting during wartime was called *recolage* and recruiting officers could be just as ruthless and underhanded as their British counterparts. Some of those recruits who joined the army whilst under the influence of alcohol would seek to desert when they sobered up to discover what they had done. When caught they were punished, usually by flogging. This was often done in front of the man's regiment and it was a drummer who had the unenviable task of administering the punishment. It was a drummer who had attracted the man to enlist and, on realising he did not want to serve and deserted, it was a drummer who punished him, which could not have endeared the drummer to the soldier. To some it could appear like some kind of perverse existence unique to military service. Not all recruits were reluctant, such as John Shipp who joined the ranks on seeing the recruiting party with its '… drums beating, colours flying…'.

Recruiting into the British army always produced good results in Ireland in terms of numbers, probably because the men wished to escape the poor existence they faced and the army at least offered food and money. In 1830 about 42 per cent of the soldiers in the British army came from Ireland and even in 1861, when living conditions had improved to some degree, the numbers of Irish serving in the ranks still accounted for more than 28 per cent. In 1775 a recruiting party comprising of a certain Major Roche equipped with 'a large purse of gold' was accompanied by a Captain Cowley and proceeded to make its way through a part of Ireland to 'drum up' recruits. As the group went they attracted 'a great number of likely recruits' and they had with them 'an elegant band of music consisting of French Horns, Hautboys, Clarionets and Bassoons playing "God Save the King"'. In keeping with tradition, the whole group was escorted by 'a large brewer's dray with five barrels of beer … two draymen, with cockades, to serve the beer'. Alcohol was being freely given to those interested in an effort to convince them to join the army. For those who 'took the King's shilling…' the party had a 'recruiting sergeant. Drums and fifes [and] another division of recruits'. The spectacle was probably repeated all over the United Kingdom. At the same time as this recruiting party was trawling for prospective soldiers, the first moves in the American War of Independence were being fought. Those who were classed as fit enough would be sent across the Atlantic to fight in this war after basic training – many of them would not return. In 1812 Sergeant Thomas Jackson of the Coldstream Guards was trying to gather interest with his recruiting party by taking '… a drum and fife, and [to] attend all the wakes, races and revels within twenty miles of London'. The recruiters had to wear their best uniforms and tell tales of glory and honour, but Sergeant Jackson was not at ease in this role like Captain Blackadder ninety-seven years earlier, although he had to carry out his mission because an order was and order and any dereliction of his duty could lead to his being reduced to the ranks and possibly even flogged for refusing.

In that same year an inspection of troops of the 51st Regiment of Foot (later to become the King's Own Yorkshire Light Infantry) was taking place on the Mediterranean island of Minorca where the officers were found to be 'properly armed … clothed according to the regulation'. The sergeant and corporals were reported as being 'in general old [but] of a soldier-like appearance'. The other ranks were noted as being 'robust and active' while the Drums and Fifes 'beat and play well, and are good looking young men, and a great ornament to the regiment'. The regiment would serve at the Battle of Waterloo in 1815 and gain a number of battle honours which would be painted onto the drums of the regiment. Another acquisition had been made by the British in the Mediterranean when Gibraltar was captured in July 1704, thereby safeguarding the entrance into the Mediterranean for the Royal Navy. The commanding officer, Sir George Rooke, took the surrender of the Spanish commander, the Marquess de Salines, who marched out of the garrison at the head of his troops with 'drums beating and colours flying'.

As we have seen, drummers were used to relay signals and attract attention to draw men in to the recruiting stations. From this we derive the expressions 'drumming up interest' and 'drumming up support', terms which today we use quite freely, but originally they meant to call the troops at meal time or other parades such as to witness punishment or to signal the alert if the camp was believed to be under attack. Sentries would call out for the drummer to sound the alert or even messengers hurrying in from further afield. For example, on the night of 5 July 1685, the eve of the Battle of Westonzoyland, a trooper in the king's army rode into camp calling out: 'Beat your drums, the enemy has come. For the Lord's sake beat your drums.' His cries were to warn of the night approach of the rebel army. His warning was timely and the rebel army was defeated because the drummers had been quick to beat out the alarm signal for the troops to assemble for battle. Captain MacKintosh, serving in the Scots regiment, was also alert to the approaching enemy and called out that the drummers in his regiment were to 'beat up their drums' in alarm, which they repeated at least twenty times to turn out the whole encampment in readiness to challenge the rebel forces.

At the start of the fourteenth century, music was becoming more familiar as a feature among the military as fifes, bugles and trumpets played to keep the troops marching in unison and to maintain morale, along with the beat of drums. Trumpets were being used to relay signals to the troops, especially in their camps. By the time of the Burgundian Wars of 1474–1477, the first regular military bands were being established by the mercenary forces of the Swiss Cantons, whose reputation in battle was highly respected. The Chronicles of the Swiss city of Basle for 1332 records the use of drums and fifes, and in 1492 the Privy Purse for King Henry VII of England notes how a payment of £2 was made for twenty-two *Sweches Grete Tabors*. These were large drums of Swiss design, indicating that the country was recognised for its drums, and the instruments were either being brought into the country directly from Switzerland or Swiss drum-makers travelled to England to make the instruments. The term *Sweche* can be found repeated in records relating to drums and music of around this time and is used to refer to the instruments used to play 'Sweche music'. The Swiss mercenary groups were organised into units known as *Banners* and these were sub-divided in

smaller groups called *Fahnlein*, which had a strength of anywhere from fifty men
to perhaps as many as 150 men. The *Banner*, being the largest formation, was usually accompanied on the march by musicians who played the drum and fife, and
these were paid for by the unit's commanding officer. Although the Swiss mercenaries had a formidable reputation, their loyalty could soon disappear if they were
not paid. It was frequently said that: 'When the money runs out so do the Swiss'.
However, it was not only the Swiss who did this, because any mercenary force
would only fight for those who could pay the highest.

Germanic mercenaries, known as *Landsknechte*, engaged in the Burgundian
Wars are understood to have used drums and these may have been copied
from Swiss mercenaries. From around 1494 onwards, during the reign of King
Francois I, the use of the fife spread throughout the French army and within fifty
years the first drums are properly recorded in the country, being called *tambourini*.
The shells were made from wood and measured some 24in in diameter and were
carried on the left hand side of the player. The Swiss and *Landsknechte* fought side
by side under the French commander Gaston de Poix at the Battle of Ravenna in
1512 against the Spanish, and so each unit would have been familiar with drums
on the battlefield. It was a hard-fought battle and eventually the French, with
their mercenaries, defeated the Spanish. Fifes and drums were now being supplied by the French ordnance and although defeated the Spanish army would
have been aware of the drummers on the battlefield, possibly leading to the further influence of their use in battle. Within fifty years of the Battle of Ravenna
the Regiment of the Gardes Francaises (French Guard) was raised in 1563 with
musicians attached. The trend had been set and, once established, it was only a
question of time before the demand for martial music to accompany a military
force spread, as with all such fashions for things martial. According to the musical historian Canon Francis Galpini, the drum was introduced to England from
Spain. The drum was known at the English Royal Court in the early fourteenth
century, probably brought over by returning Crusaders passing through Spain.
The point had been reached where the first military bands in Europe were being
established for the specific purpose of accompanying troops on the march.

The Swiss association with the earliest martial music was maintained by the
regiment of the Swiss Guards, dating back to 1506 when Pope Julius ordered
the raising of a company of 150 men from the Canton of Zurich, and this was
very much a fighting force. Some European monarchs raised similar groups from
Swiss cantons, including one for the French Royal Household in 1640, which
is recorded as having a drum and fife attached to each company. The term *tabor*
or *tabrett* starts to appear to be replaced, certainly in the English language, by the
term *drome*, *dromme* or *drume* from where we obviously today derive the word
drum. By 1665 this strength had increased in number by three more drums. The
number of drums would later be reduced, but by 1692 it was reported in the
French publication *Mercure Galant* that at the Siege of Namur the Swiss Guards

had some forty drums for signalling purposes. The *Mercure Galant* was first published between 1674 and 1677 and although it would have breaks in publication
throughout the eighteenth century, it continued in print into the early nienteenth
century. Sometimes known by a slightly different name, the reporting published
in the *Mercure Galant* gave an insight into the events of the day and what was
fashionable at the time, including military trends.

The Siege of Namur, as reported in the *Mercure Galant*, was an episode in the
period known as the Nine Years' War or War of the Grand Alliance (1688–1697)
and involved France facing its old adversary England, which was in alliance with
the Dutch Republic and the Holy Roman Empire. The French had captured the
city of Namur, in modern-day Belgium, in 1692 and held it until the Allied forces
besieged it in early 1695. During the siege both sides encountered heavy losses
before the French finally surrendered on 1 September. What is interesting about
the action is that present at the siege were a number of famous English regiments,
which would become renowned for their regimental bands. This included the
future Grenadier and Coldstream Guards, which was raised in 1650 and known
to have a regimental band and drummers by 1742. Illustrations showing drums
being played at special events begin to appear around the start of the sixteenth
century, such as the painting by Vittore Carpaccio depicting Turkish drummers,
and provide evidence that people were becoming familiar with the instrument
across Europe. The painting by Joannes van Duetecum in 1558 shows musicians
playing drums and trumpets at the funeral of Charles V.

The martial use of the drum was spreading quickly and becoming increasingly
popular, and not just with military commanders. For example, in 1622 the historian Francis Markham wrote in his work 'Five Decades of Epistles of Warre' how:
'It is the voice of the Drum the souldier should wholly attend'. He rebukes the
use of the fife by stating that: "The phiph is but onlie an instrument of Pleasure,
not of necessitie…' He was supported in this belief by Sir John Turner, who
wrote in his work 'Pallas Armata' over sixty years later that he did not consider the
fife very important, although, despite this opinion, that: 'In some places a piper
(fifer) is allowed for each company…' This was in the style of the Swiss Guard of
the mid-century period. The drum on the other hand was considered extremely
important; an opinion reinforced a number of times by writers of the time, such
as Gervase Markham.

The French writer on music Thoinot Arbeau described the French drum
of the mid-seventeenth century as measuring some 30in in diameter, with the
shell enclosed at both ends and buff cords to brace or tension the skin. Other
drums from the period are recorded with similar measurements and are known
to have been played by drummers using two sticks, as shown in paintings such as
'The Night Watch' by Rembrandt in 1642. The sticks had rounded ends and this
allowed drummers to beat distinct signals more easily, such as the 'double beat'
which over time developed into the 'drum roll'. The height of the drum itself

by 1790 was almost unchanged, but the diameter for some styles had increased considerably to 42in. It is also recorded at this time that boys *enfants de troupe* (children of the troop) as young as 7 years old were being recruited as drummers into the French army. With the political union between Scotland and England, the term 'British Army' was created and, like its French counterpart, it had no compunctions when it came to accepting very young boys into its ranks, as illustrated by an Inspection Return for the 7th Dragoon Guards in 1788, which states that one of the regiment's trumpeters was '... too young and too little to mount a horse...' In this case things were taken too far, but boys as young as 10 years old were taken into the army to serve as drummers or trumpeters, and instances of some even younger, perhaps aged as little as 7 years old, were recorded. It may seem harsh by today's standards to send such young boys to serve in the army and fight in war, but it should be remembered that for large families where food was scarce, this option at least allowed one member of the family to be fed. It would not be until 1844 that Queen's Regulations changed the British army's policy on young boys serving in the ranks and a limit of 14 years of age was imposed for enlistment. Even so, young drummer boys would continue to serve and die in the campaigns of the British Empire in Africa and India. The list of drummers in action during the Battle of Waterloo with the 23rd Regiment of Foot on 18 June 1815 records that one was 18 years of age and one was 62 years of age. Many of the 23rd Regiments drummers were under 18 when they enlisted.

Music was very rarely written down as a musical score during this period and certainly almost unknown for drums. It is most likely that music, techniques and rhythm would have been passed on by one drummer to another. Arbeau writes on this method of teaching: '... our Frenchmen drummers are instructed to make the rankers and bondsmen of the squadrons march to certain rhythms. In marching, if three men are walking together, and each one moves at a different speed, they will not be in step, because to be so they must all three march in unison, either quickly, moderately or slowly...' He continues on the subject: 'The French make use of the drum to beat the rhythm to which soldiers must march. A drum rhythm contains minims (tans) of which the first five are beaten'. He describes how this is done by the drummer hitting '... the first four with one tap of the stick, and the fifth with two sticks together, and the other three beats are silent. The left foot must be put down on the first note, and the right on the fifth...' It sounds complicated, but it becomes clear as Arbeau explains that: '... if all eight notes were struck, a soldier could put down his feet on notes other than the first or fifth notes'. He calculates that in such a way, a group of soldiers marching for 2,500 drum beats can cover a distance of a league, approximately 3 miles, in a smart and efficient manner.

During the reign of Queen Mary Tudor of England (1553–1558), Jack Hawkins, writing under the pseudonym of Ralph Smith, recorded how: 'All captains must have drums and fifes and men to use the same, who shall be faithful, secret and ingenious, of able personage to use their instruments and office of sundry languages; for often-times they be sent to parley with their enemies, to summon their towns and forts, to redeem and conduct prisoners and divers other messages, which of necessity requireth language. If such drums or fifes should fortune fall into the hands of the enemies, no gift no force should cause them to disclose any secret that they know. They must oft practise their instruments, teach the company the sound of the march, alarm, approach, assault, battle, retreat, skirmish, or any other calling that of necessity should be known. They must be obedient to the commandant of the captain and ensign, when they shall command them to come and go or stand, or sound their retreat or other calling.' This tells us that the drummer had great responsibility and was in a position of trust. Not only did he have to be able to teach his musical technique and converse in foreign languages, but he also had to be trustworthy if taken captive. The description also points out that drummers by their very privileged position would know things not known to ordinary soldiers of the rank and file. If he were captured and threatened by torture to reveal these, he was expected to maintain his silence. He should also be beyond reproach and not tempted by bribery to reveal any secrets. It was a position of rank and status, but it came at the high price of what was expected of him.

In 1521 Niccolo Machiavelli opined in his work *Art of War* that the drum commands all things in a battle by conveying the orders of an officer to his troops. Seventy years later, the writer William Garrard in his identically entitled book, albeit with different spelling, *Arte of Warre*, states that on the stroke of a drum '... the soldier shall go, just and even, with a gallant and sumptuous pace...' In the eighteenth century the marching column of the French army was organised so that it was headed by regimental pioneers, followed by the artillery, with the drums and fifes and band coming behind them and in front of the marching infantry. This meant that the regiments '... arrived to the sound of their bands...' and could not have been achieved if the drummer or his position were not highly regarded and respected.

Works written in the early part of the seventeenth century were only reconfirming the role of the drummer and his position which, although not entirely neglected, was now being rediscovered after many centuries and was being re-evaluated. It is from around this time that some of the earliest printed regulations and instructions for a drummer begin to appear and, although this had been known about hundreds of year before, more than a passing reference is attached to his military importance.

DRUMMERS IN THE
SEVENTEENTH CENTURY

By the beginning of the seventeenth century, drums of varying sizes were in widespread use in armies all across Europe, with commanders using them to relay orders over distance. Battles were being fought by armies of ever-increasing size and the fighting was beginning to cover large areas. The use of gunpowder weapons such as muskets, but especially artillery, had caused the widening of the battlefield and the depth was also increased. For example, at the Battle of Ayn Jalut on 3 September 1260 between the Mongols and Egyptian Mamelukes, the battle frontage was 5,000yds wide. Both sides used drummers to relay signals and some very early hand cannons, known as *midfa*, may have been used. At the Battle of Towton on 29 March 1461 during the Wars of the Roses, gunpowder artillery was used and the depth of the battlefield measured around 1.5 miles deep. At the Battle of Austerlitz on 2 December 1805 the depth of the battlefield had extended to 10.5 miles. At the battles of Borodino and Waterloo, 1812 and 1815 respectively, the battlefields stretched over many miles and drums were used for signalling, morale and to keep the troops on the move. To issue verbal commands over such distances would have been impossible and the mêlée of the battle, now with the added noise of gunfire, would have drowned out any audible meaning. Flags and banners had long been used as rallying points for troops and while these were still used as a focal point for troops to muster round on the battlefield as they formed into regiments, the bugle and drum relayed the signals to charge and reform. As the late historian David Chandler points out in his book *The Art of Warfare on Land*, it was the drummer who '... served to transmit orders during the din of battle'.

Written commands and other messages could be conveyed from a commander's position to a field unit by a rider, but the trouble with that was if the messenger was shot or captured the message was lost or fell into the hands of the enemy. Furthermore, it could happen that by the time such a written message was dispatched and received the situation it related to could have changed, meaning that the communication would have lost all its significance. This was the kind of thing that contributed to the disastrous Charge of the Light Brigade on

25 October 1854 during the Crimean War. The British commander, Lord Raglan, realised that the Russians were trying to remove captured Turkish artillery from the field and ordered the Light Brigade, an elite cavalry force, to prevent this from happening. Written orders were conveyed to Lord Cardigan by Captain Nolan, but the message was misinterpreted and lead to the ill-fated charge during which Captain Nolan was killed.

Drums, therefore, remained the only solution to all of these problems and, on being beaten, it was almost certain that all could hear the command signals which would be relayed by other drummers taking up the call. In this way the troops across the battlefield would act on the moment the signal was recognised. At least one large field drum was to be found within every company of infantry and the members of this unit would have been familiar to the command signals being beaten out, which were known as the 'Calls of Warre'. The troops would have known to advance, withdraw or hold position with these certain signals. If new recruits within the unit were unfamiliar with the signals then they would have followed the example set by the older, more experienced troops as they reacted to the drum beats.

An army on the march kept pace at a rhythm tapped out by drummers, who were often experienced veterans of campaigns and as such were men rather than the drummer 'boys' of later periods. Drummers in the seventeenth century often held the rank of either corporal or sergeant and were distinct from the rank and file. An account from 1598 records that a corporal was '...a degree in dignitie above the private soldier...' Almost fifty years later, Sergeant Nehemiah Wharton, who served in the Parliamentarian army, referred to non-commissioned officers and officers in his writings as 'we officers' to denote their status. Although not officer status, their unique position as drummers placed them above the ordinary infantryman and in some armies were actually afforded recognition of officer status, even though they did not hold an officer's commission. In view of their importance and prominence, drummers had to be steady, reliable men, not given easily to retreating without receiving the order directly from his commander to relay the signal. Even then a drummer had to stand his ground to beat out the signal to retreat before he too could withdraw. If he deserted his post then a commander had in effect lost his voice to issue orders and the army would have been severely compromised. In the event of any drummer being caught after such an action, he would almost certainly have been executed on the spot for his cowardice. Drummers stood their ground along with the troops and had to accept the fact that they could become casualties.

Sergeant Nehemiah Wharton had been keeping a written account of his service with the Parliamentarian army since the outbreak of the English Civil War in 1642 and his account of an early skirmish or minor engagement tells how drummers became victims in the fighting. He writes: 'In the morning our enemies, consisting of about 800 horse and 300 foot, with ordnance, led by the Earl of Northampton, the Lord of Carnarvon, and the Lord Compton and Captain Legge, and others, intended to set upon us before we could gather our companies together; but being ready all night, early in the morning we went to meet them with a few troops of horse and six field pieces [artillery]; and being on fire to be at them we marched through the corn and got the hill of them, whereupon they played upon us with their ordnance, but they came short. Our gunner took their own bullet, sent it to them again, and killed a horse and a man. After we gave them eight shot more, whereupon all their foot companies fled.' The exchange of fire here tells us that it was not a planned attack, but more of a surprise engagement by two forces who reacted to the moment. The Royalist gunners trying to fire uphill led to the cannon balls falling short and the Parliamentarian gunners using them against the Royalist troops with telling effect. Nehemiah Wharton continues his description of the encounter: 'The number of men slain, as themselves report, was fifty beside horses. One drummer being dead at the bottom of the hill, our knapsack boys rifled to the shirt, which was very lousy. Another drummer we found two miles off with his arm shot off, and lay a-dying. Several dead corpses we found in the field, and amongst them a trumpeter, whose trumpet our horsemen sounded into Coventry…' This record informs us how the drummers were exposed to musket fire and how, despite their non-combatant status, they could still expect to be killed in the general confusion of battle. The fact that the dead drummer's corpse was going to be looted along with the other dead, but was left due to the filthy condition of his shirt, tells us that there were limits to what men were prepared to accept even among the hardship of war.

Drummers were given many privileges besides status and were sometimes present during important discussions between the commanders of opposing armies, having first signalled that his officers wished to 'parley' (after the French term *parlez* – to speak). Some sources believe that because drummers would enter enemy camps during such meetings to help organise the conferences, they could use their position to spy on enemy forces. If this was true and their intentions were discovered, they would have risked being arrested and executed for spying and abusing the trust placed with them. It would also have meant that the rank of drummer would never be trusted again, as the word of even one act of spying would have universally tarnished the reputation of drummers and they would never have been tolerated in such an important role ever again. This was an opinion held as early as 1622 by Francis Markham, who wrote in his work 'Five Decades of Epistles of Warre' that: 'No gifte or force should cause him [the drummer] to disclose any secret he knows'.

It is quite possible that some drummers of this period who may have seen service overseas, possibly as a mercenary during one of the protracted wars such as the Thirty Years' War (1618–1648), the English Civil War (1642–1650) and later conflicts including the Great Northern War (1700–1720) and the Seven

Years' War (1756–1763), may have acquired some knowledge of a foreign language such as French, Spanish, English or Dutch. Gervase Markham wrote in 1643 that a drummer must be '... gentle and of great respect, a good linguist and take notice of such things of importance as shall encounter his eyes and ear...' Skills, such as being able to speak a foreign language, would almost certainly have elevated a drummer's position of importance during parleys and one which he would certainly not abuse by undertaking any form of subversive or clandestine act. However, that is not to say that out of loyalty a drummer could not furnish his commander a more general view of things he had seen in the enemy's camp, such as numbers of troops and the state of morale. It was considered un-gentlemanly to kill a drummer, or indeed any observer, attending the course of a parley even if he was accused of spying. Arrest and trial or at least ejection from the procedures of parley would have been the first course of action. According to one set of 'Articles of War', which governs the conduct of a country's military forces in time of war, when concerning the matter of parley it says: '... none shall speak with a Drum or Trumpet or any other sent by the Enemy without order upon pain of punishment at discretion...' The punishment for infringing this directive could be a flogging, which in turn would be administered by a drummer and can be seen as a perverse irony.

Parleys were conducted on many occasions during the Civil War, one of which was recorded as taking place during the siege of Sherborne Castle in Dorset during August 1645. The siege was a short but fierce and bloody affair, which some sources claim lasted eleven days, whilst others claim the castle withstood the siege for as long as fifteen days. Oliver Cromwell described Sherborne Castle as '...malicious and mischievous...' It had been attacked in 1642 and although the Royalist garrison, commanded by Sir Thomas Lunsford, had stood firm, they eventually gave way to a far stronger force of attackers, commanded by the Earl of Bedford, and the castle was surrendered. There is much debate about whether the castle was taken or, as some sources claim, that the defenders held firm and the Royalists remained in charge of the castle after the attackers abandoned the siege on 6 September. However, English Heritage, which manages the site of the castle, and the local historical society and museum all state the castle did surrender to Parliamentarian forces in 1642. The second siege was to be very different and the commander of the Parliamentarian forces, Sir Thomas Fairfax, was determined to capture the castle once and for all. He ordered up the siege train of artillery from Portsmouth to reduce the walls of the castle and the great guns duly arrived at the site on 11 August. The castle dated back to the twelfth century and its stout walls, whilst offering protection against musket fire, would not withstand a pounding by artillery and were further weakened by mining.

After four days of artillery bombardment the commander of the castle garrison, Sir Lewis Dyves (sometimes written as Dives), realised that to continue to defend the castle would be futile. At around 2am on 15 August he sent a drummer with a message to parley with Sir Thomas Fairfax, communicating that he was prepared to surrender if given honourable terms. Sir Thomas became angry at the suggestion, probably knowing full well it was only a question of time before the garrison had to surrender without discussing terms. Still, protocol had to be followed.

Sir Thomas sent his own drummer to convey his reply to Sir Lewis in the castle. The drummer bearing the message would have been aware of the strong position his commanding officer was in and this may have caused him to become over-confident in his manner, so that when he came to deliver Sir Thomas' message the drummer's attitude was discernable and caused Sir Lewis to fly into a rage and almost order the drummer to be hanged. However, he knew the man was under the protection of the terms of parley and he had to restrain himself.

Sherborne Castle surrendered later that day and Anne Finch, Countess of Winchilsea (1661–1720) later wrote of the affair in one of her poems: 'Trail all your pikes, dispirit every drum, March in long procession from afar ye silent, ye dejected men of war! Be still the hautboys, let the flute be dumb.' Garrisons could march out of castles following the agreement of terms concluding a siege, as happened at Conwy Castle in North Wales, where after a three-month siege in 1646 the Royalist garrison marched out with '… drums beating and colours flying…' When Raglan Castle in South Wales surrendered on 19 August in the same year, the Royalist garrison was permitted to march out with '… colours flying, drums beating and trumpets sounding…' They were more fortunate than the garrison of Basing House in Hampshire where most of the garrison had been put to the sword following the siege a year before. Drummers had served as messengers during this action and had been used to carry messages and relay orders, among other duties. In most cases, though, such surrendered castles, including Sherborne, were 'slighted', which is to say that they were destroyed so as to render them no longer useful as a point of resistance or to house a garrison. The besieged Royalist garrison at Donnington Castle near Newbury in Berkshire surrendered in March 1646 following a parley arranged through drummers. The garrison commander, Colonel John Boys, was allowed to march out at the head of 200 men, '… with bagge and baggage, musckets charged and primed, mache in Coke, bullate in mouth, drums beating and Collurers fleyinge'. This was the due honours of war credited to men who had fought well. The castle was destroyed, but the Parliamentarians captured gunpowder and artillery which strengthened their army and denied it to the Royalists.

Three years earlier in August 1642, drummers had been used to negotiate a parley during the siege of the harbour town of Portsmouth. The town had been invested by the Earl of Warwick, who established a naval blockade at sea whilst Parliamentarian forces built positions on land to ensure the town remained cut off from reinforcements. Over the next three weeks more preparations were made to bombard the town and artillery positions were established in the surrounding area.

The Royalist garrison under the command of Lord Goring realised the helpless-ness of their situation and sent out a drummer on 4 September to discuss terms. Three days later, terms having been agreed, the siege was lifted and Portsmouth surrendered, saving it from bombardment and almost certain destruction. This gave the Parliamentarian forces a vital naval port and denied it to the Royalist forces of King Charles I, who could not use it for moving troops and supplies.

Drummers could also be used to help in deciding the outcome of an engage-ment by their actions, despite the fact they were non-combatant in what could be called 'passive resistance'. At the siege of Sandal Castle at Wakefield in West Yorkshire during 1645, Sir John Savile had been entrusted with the action by Sir Thomas Fairfax. The Parliamentarian forces believed their position was strong, but they would come to find themselves outwitted partially by the actions of the drummers from within the castle. One Sunday, upon hearing what he believed to be the drummers of the castle calling the garrison to prayers, Sir John Savile allowed his troops to relax their vigilance and continue with their own religious observations. The Royalist troops commanded by Colonel Bonivant, governor of the castle, ordered his men to attack at this moment. The garrison had heard the '… rebels beat their drummers to praiers…' and seizing the opportunity to attack, once they had lowered their guard, surged out of the castle gates. The attack so surprised the Parliamentarian forces that Savile was forced to retreat, with forty-two men having been killed in the assault and a further fifty taken prisoner. The siege had been lifted, but in October 1645 the Parliamentarians once more besieged Sandal Castle and this time succeeded in capturing it. The castle was systematically destroyed by 'slighting' to prevent it from being used as a military or civilian base.

Armies of this period were also adopting the wearing of a uniform to distin-guish one from the other and drummers had to wear this as they went about their duties. During the English Civil War the Parliamentarian forces wore orange sashes to identify them in battle, while the Royalists preferred white for the same reason. To further distinguish one side from the other and even individual units, coloured jackets were adopted. For example, the Royalist troops under the com-mand of Colonel Paulet wore yellow jackets and Parliamentarian troops under John Hampden wore green jackets. This fashion extended to drummers, some of whom may have gone a stage further and adopted more flamboyant styles to stand out. However, in so doing they would have drawn attention to them-selves, becoming targets for musketeers who would have deliberately aimed at them in the knowledge that if the drummers were killed then the passing of orders through the army would have become extremely difficult. A precedent for this colourful fashion in uniforms had been set many years earlier and even during the reign of Queen Elizabeth I of England the army wore a range of col-ours, including the '… Queen's colours of white and green…' Red also proved a popular colour and this can still be seen in the modern British army, with the

Guards regiments wearing scarlet tunics for ceremonial parades such as Trooping the Colour, and the drummers also wearing a special style with 'swallows nests' extensions on their shoulders.

In the seventeenth century, drummers typically carried their drums suspended from either a broad leather strap or a brightly coloured sash worn over the right shoulder, with the drum resting high up on the left hip. On most occasions this would be the side drum, which was carried at an angle to hang at around 45 degrees. The larger drums, referred to as *nakers*, were carried on a man's back, whilst the drummer walked behind to beat them. Later these would be carried on the chest and become the bass drum. A variation was developed to be suspended from harnesses fitted to horses, known as kettledrums, and were used by cavalry regiments. The *naker* style of drum carried on a man's back was also known in sixteenth-century Japan and illustrations show them being played in a similar manner.

Despite the fact that a drummer's status on the battlefield was non-combatant, he could be armed with at least a sword for self-defence as this did not contravene his status because he should be allowed to defend himself. Admittedly there are those who would argue that a battlefield is no place for a non-combatant, but drummers are first and foremost soldiers and therefore their place is in line with other troops. There is some debate as to whether the sword was worn suspended from a belt on the left or the right side in such circumstances. There are some contemporary illustrations showing both styles, but one has to question if this is a true representation or if the artist at the time automatically assumed that a drummer in the army would be armed. However, when put to the test with modern re-enactors, we can see how difficult it would have been for a drummer to draw his sword to protect himself if he had to. If the sword was worn on the left side, it would have been covered by his drum and not immediately accessible. If the sword was worn on the right side, assuming the man was right-handed, it would have been impossible to draw the weapon clear from its scabbard. This leaves two trains of thought on the matter. Firstly, that the sword may have been carried as another status symbol, something that continued through the Victorian period when drummers in the British army carried long-bladed, sword bayonets, and continues today, with drummers in the Guards Regiments still carrying bayonets for the modern SA-80 rifle. The second thought is that the artist was only painting or drawing what he believed was the case, without actually having seen a fully equipped drummer turned out for parade. The typical case in point is an illustration appearing in the 1625 work 'Double-armed Man' by William Neade, showing a man shooting a longbow and holding a pike at the same time. This has been proven to be an impossible task by recreating the scene with modern re-enactors, who show conclusively that a bow and pike could not be held together in the same hand. There is only one conclusion to draw from such illustrations and that is the artist was drawing what he thought was correct without any proper knowledge of the subject.

Despite the ravages of time and disasters such as fires, floods and wars, an incredible number of examples of seventeenth-century drums have survived around the world. Not all have been kept in conditions conducive to their particular drumhead fabric, but modern conservation techniques and museum staff, skilled in the art of preservation and restoration, have reversed and halted further decay. These surviving drums are now preserved and from them we can see an incredible degree of commonality, not only in the painted decorative designs, but also the way in which they were constructed. Many are between 20 and 22in in diameter and have an average depth of 25in. If smaller drums were used then we do not have any examples, either because they did not exist or have not survived the ravages of time.

The shell, or body, and the hoops of these drums are wooden, often made of oak, but some are of other hard, durable type woods, with the heads being of calf skin and in some examples made of goat skin. The uppermost, or top, skin is referred to as the 'batter' head, because it was struck with sticks or 'battered', while the underside skin is called the 'snare' head and is usually formed from a thinner covering of leather. These heads were tensioned by means of ropes passing through the hoops. Some examples are fitted with a snare made from animal gut and, depending on its tension, could create a distinct noise which would have sounded like 'buzzing' to those hearing it from behind.

The shell of these drums invariably have at least one small hole bored into it; a feature which some have identified as being ventilation to allow the natural animal skin used in the heads to 'breathe' and so prevent a build-up of moisture, which would lead to the formation of mildew and cause the drum to rot. Examples of drum shells show they were decorated with painted motifs and other designs of either political or religious significance. Some have been decorated by brass pins being tapped into the shell to form a pattern. Close examination of examples have revealed that some have been redecorated by painting over the original design. This indicates that captured drums were either used to replace those destroyed in battle or to increase the number of drums in a unit, with the new owners redecorating the drums to their taste. Not all were decorated so intricately and shells do exist which have simply been oiled or waxed to preserve them from the effects of the weather.

Armies of the seventeenth century were made up of four different elements: the cavalry, the infantry with muskets, artillery and the pike block, which was used to good effect to break up cavalry charges by presenting a wall of spikes protruding up to 18ft in length. On the battlefield, drummers were often positioned with such a formation and up to two drummers could be stationed with each company of pikemen. These troops, and the weapon they handled, were considered honourable and this reputation reflected well on the drummers serving within the pike block because of their individual position within an army. Using the pike required strength and a pikeman had to be sturdy, characteristics often associated with drummers, and so they can be seen to compliment each other by being in the same company.

Drummers were required to sound a range of instructions not only on the battlefield and route of march, but also around the camp in general. A single signal beaten on the drum was far more audible and readily understandable than a babble arousing from a multitude of voices all shouting at different points. Writing in 1661, William Barriffe records in his work 'Militarie Discipline' that: '... the Drum is the voice of the Commander...' There were drum beats or 'Calls to Warre' for just about every occasion with several more common calls. Firstly, the drummers would beat out the 'Assembly', which had a two-fold purpose: when sounded in camp it signalled that the troops were to form up in ranks and file by their Regimental Colours in preparation to march; when sounded on the battlefield it meant that the troops should rally and reform if the unit had become spread out and disorganised during the fighting.

Versions of such signals obviously differed from one country to the next and, even with the signal to 'March', the English, Scots, French and various German states, including Prussia and Hanover, each had their own signal for this movement. Drummers, by their very nature, were flamboyant and often given to extravagant flourishes on the drum, sometimes referred to in modern times as 'twiddly bits'. These were used to liven up the tempo because, as with the English march which is recorded as '... frankly quite boring...' troops needed something to stimulate them. In 1702 a journalist by the name of Nathaniel Crouch, who for some reason wrote under the *nom de plume* of either Richard or Robert Burton, recounted a conversation on this topic in his work 'Admirable Curiosities and Wonders of England'. He tells how, during the course of a conversation, the French Marshal Baron de Biron said of the English drum-march to his English counterpart Sir Roger Williams, who had written 'A Brief Discours on War', that in his opinion it was too slow and sluggish. To which Sir Roger responded by saying: 'Slow it is, but it has traversed your Master's country from one end to the other'. The discussion between these two men happened sometime during the reign of Queen Elizabeth I of England and certainly before July 1592, as the unfortunate Baron de Biron was killed at that time during the Siege of Epernay.

Forty years after the death of the Baron de Biron and ten years before the outbreak of the English Civil War, a warrant decreed by King Charles I of England was issued in 1632 governing the method of marching to the beat of the drum in which it is stated that: 'Whereas the ancient customs of nations hath ever beene to use one certain and constant forme of March in the warres, whereby to be distinguished from one another. And the March of this our nation [England], so famous in all the honourable achievements and glorious warres of this our kingdom in forraigne parts (being by the approbation of strangers confest and acknowledged the best of all marches) was through the negligence and carelessness of drummers, and by long discontinuance so altered and changed from the ancient gravity and majestic thereof, as it was in danger utterly to have beene lost and forgotten. It pleased our late dear brother prince Henry to revive and rectifie the same ordering an establishment of one certain measure, which was beaten at his presence at Greenwich anno 1610.' This was clearly a move to prevent the complete loss of the order and pace of troops marching as a unit, and to reverse any deficiencies that may have crept in over the years. Marching as a complete force was obviously recognised as a way of keeping the unit together and also for instilling discipline.

This was not the only word on the matter of troops marching to the beat of the drum. The anonymous author of the work entitled 'Warlike Directions or the Soldier's Practice', dating from around 1643 when the English Civil War was barely one year in the fighting, writes:'I have thought mete for the benefit of each Drummer which is not yet perfect in the March, to prick down the old English March newly revised in the plainest forme I could invent. Wishing that all drummers would leave off other forms invented, either by themselves, or others herein unskilled that there may be a uniformitie in this kingdom, as in all other nation'. The author is clearly making a call to standardise the marching beat to avoid confusing the troops, who at the time of writing were often labourers or other manual workers who would not have been able to read and write and would have had to be trained very quickly and simply in their duties as a soldier during the Civil War. This extended to instruction to determine a man's left hand and his right hand, such was the low level of a man's education at the time. It would not be for another two years, in 1643, that the Parliamentarian forces would raise the New Model Army, the first professional military force in the country with something approaching a proper training regime.

Knowing how monotonous the act of marching could be, the drummers would often introduce changes to liven it up, which the troops enjoyed because they were different. It was also a drummer's way of showing off his skills, although it was not always appreciated and during the English Civil War King Charles forbade his drummers from making such performances. As Sir James Turner wrote in his work 'Pallas Armata' of 1683, that if a drummer can '… convey a message wittily to an enemy he may be permitted to be Droll, as Doctors is a thing that is not at all required by his hands'. This says much about the cavalier manner of drummers on the battlefield as well as off it during the sending and receiving of messages between opposing sides.

On the battlefield itself the drummers would beat out the 'Voluntary', which was a general signal for all troops to prepare themselves. For example, the pikemen would stand with pikes held upright and musketeers would load their weapons in the front rank, presenting their muskets by placing them on the special musket rests, a monopod support which took the weight of the weapon. These musket rests would later disappear as muskets became lighter and more manageable. This signal was usually followed by 'Company will prepare to march by Column of Divisions'. On hearing this, each unit would move into its designated position on the battlefield ready for

the fight. The signal of the *Battaile* was the equivalent of the 'Charge' and the pikemen in particular would 'charge their pikes' by holding them horizontally towards
the enemy and moving forward to close the gap. This tactic has come to be known
as the 'push of pike' and at the Battle of Worcester (1651) Oliver Cromwell wrote:
'... the dispute was very long, and very near at hand, and often at push of pike...'
Use of the pike required considerable strength and in Scotland the equivalent was
termed the *schiltrom* and remained in use until well into the eighteenth century
when the first bayonets came into service. Even then, commanders such as Maurice
de Saxe employed it in time-honoured tradition '... and would order his pike blocks
to advance towards the enemy lines'. The Battaile could also signal musketeers who
had fired their weapons, but not yet reloaded, that they should reverse their muskets
and use the heavy butt-stock end in a clubbing action and '... fall on the enemy...'

Another signal the drummers were required to sound on the battlefield was
'The Troop', which was used to consolidate those troops which may still be on
the march and in effect hurried the men along and 'drew them in' to the battle.
Pikemen would come to the advance and all would close up in one unit. The
order to 'Reform the Battalia' could be given verbally, but the drummers would
have been better suited for clarity and if all went according to the drill rules, the
troops would move from the marching column to form the line of battle. An army
on the march moved in a long, snaking column and, although it allowed troops
move quickly, it was not considered an effective fighting formation because it
only permitted the first three or four ranks to fire their muskets at the same time.
This limitation in firepower was overcome by moving into a formation of line
abreast, which was very wide and, although not very deep, it did allow every
man to fire his weapon at the same time on the given signal. This type of formation could also manoeuvre either end of the line at an angle to protect against
flanking attacks. In later years this tactic would be developed further to employ
a ruse known as 'refusing' the enemy: the troops would appear to withdraw and
disengage from the attackers if threatened by a column; the enemy would move
closer, believing that they had forced their adversary to retreat, when all the time
it was a feint and once committed the flanks of the line would move forward to
fire on the unprotected flanks of the attacking column. The effect was devastating
and Napoleon Bonaparte would become a master in its use.

Lastly, there was the signal to 'Retreat', although in the seventeenth century
this signal did not always necessarily mean what we understand the term to be
today, which is to depart the battlefield. On hearing the signal to Retreat, seventeenth-century troops would conduct a careful retirement in an orderly manner
and on the signal to 'Halt', they would stop and engage the advancing enemy. All
the while the drummers had to be aware of everything going on around them
and somehow survive the fighting. This tactic of retreating in such a controlled manner and reforming to return fire would not be possible if the army was
beaten and were routed from the battlefield.

Recent research has uncovered a number of other 'Calls of Warre', such as the 'Preperative', 'Parley' and the 'Allarum', each of which is quite self-explanatory, but have deeper meanings. It is not known whether or not all men knew and recognised each of these signals, as the ordinary rank and file troops, very often conscripts straight from farms, may have only learned to respond to the important signals such as march and advance. It is generally taken that as long as the officers and NCOs knew the other signals then they could respond to them and make things go to plan by directing the men in their unit. Soldiers marched to the drum beat and some officers would pay to hire other musicians to play the fife and flute to add to the tempo, but these were not soldiers and never went near the battle-field, unless they became involved by accident or during a catastrophic defeat.

The seventeenth century has come to be remembered as the period of the English Civil War, but whilst it certainly dominated events during this time, it was not the only conflict being fought. In the Far East, China and other civilisations in the region were coming into conflict with European explorers and traders, as well as rival neighbouring states. These countries fought wars of equal and some-times longer duration to those being fought in Western Europe, and with armies of comparable or greater size. On the other side of the Atlantic in the Americas, four main European countries were coming into conflict - Britain, France, Spain and Portugal - although the latter would concentrate most of its interests further south in what is modern-day Brazil. Of the three remaining countries, France and Britain would engage in open war, leading to long-term conflict which would take the fighting even further north and into Canada. The indigenous Native American tribes would take sides in these wars and, as a result, would become exposed to European-style drums; vastly different from their own primitive types, but still serving the same purpose.

Western Europe remained the hotbed of conflict during this period, with three separate Anglo-Dutch Wars being fought. The first was fought between 1652 and 1654, closely followed by the second between 1665 and 1667, and by the third fought between 1672 and 1674, when King Charles II had replaced the Commonwealth of Oliver Cromwell. On mainland Europe major conflicts broke out, as Gustavus Adolphus, king of Sweden, wrote to his Chancellor Axel Oxenstiera: 'All the wars that are on foot in Europe have been fused together, and have now become a single war'. It certainly must have seemed that way to him while writing about a conflict which was to become known as the Thirty Years' War, lasting from 1618 until 1648. Gustavus Adolphus was one of those who would not see the end of the war, being killed at the Battle of Lutzen on 16 November 1632. The Swedish army, which had set the 'model' for other European armies in the future, started each day on campaign by waking the camp and signalling the troopers to their horses by trumpet, and calling the infantry to the march by the sound of the drum. This also became standard practice among other armies and bugles still remain the method of waking the troops in some armies today, using a signal called 'Reveille' from the French word 'reveillez' meaning 'wake you up'. It is understood to have first been used in 1644 and over the years has been sounded by both drum and bugle.

Sweden went to war again between 1655 and 1660, in what has become known as the First Northern War, which saw it fighting against Russia. In England the Monmouth Rebellion was put down with bloody reprisals in 1685, but the landing of William and Mary in 1688 ousted the unpopular King James II of England in the 'Glorious Revolution'. The vastness of Europe had to be covered on foot and campaigns were measured in the miles marched by its armies. A campaign could last several months and would usually occur during the good weather months of the year, although successive military commanders, such as Napoleon Bonaparte, would extend the campaign season into the winter months. The spring and summer months were ideal for campaigning, with plenty of fodder for the horses, but a commissariat service would build logistical supply lines to keep the armies provisioned and send new recruits forward to join the ranks, making it possible to fight a war all year round.

At the Battle of Breitenfeld in 1631, according the Colonel Robert Monroe serving in the Swedish army, the fighting commenced with: '... trumpets sounding, Drummes beating and Colours advanced and flying...' There were many mercenaries finding employment during these wars, and the Swedish army of Gustavus Adolphus was no exception, with the rank filled by many Scots. During the smoke and confusion at Breitenfeld, Monroe's musketeers became disorientated and spread out. To gather them back in to form a single unit he ordered: '... a drummer by me, I caused him to beate the Scots march, till it [the smoke] cleared up which recollected our friends unto us...' It must have been a familiar beat to the troops as they gathered together for mutual support; an act which must have been repeated many times during the 'war from the Oder to the Ebro' and in the many other conflicts during this tumultuous century.

MARCHING AND DRILL

Troops in armies around the world were to be taught how to march to the beat of the drum and this training was literally 'beaten into them'. This simple expression is taken for granted today, but there was a time when it meant that drill instruction was often imparted by using a stick to beat it into the recruit. Boys could not be flogged in the army, nor could they be confined in the cells with adult soldiers, so trumpet majors and drum-majors would often punish boys by strokes of the cane to 'beat discipline into them', especially if they were without their drum when on parade. When musket drill was being given, a drummer would be on parade to beat the count between moves so that all the troops in a formation moved as one. The author, as a young guardsman at the barracks of the Guards' Depot at Pirbright in Surrey, remembers drummers being present to tap out the timings when being taught rifle drill on the parade ground. This was continuing the practise used over many centuries to make the troops move in uniformity as one and, whilst today this is purely ceremonial, it was originally intended as a display of discipline to impress the enemy. These drill movements, which had been 'beaten in' by drum, would be used later by the author when participating in the Trooping of the Colour. With the regimentation of battle tactics, which became more and more complicated in their manoeuvre, so it became increasingly important for soldiers to keep in step, and for this purpose drummers became an essential part of training within European armies. They not only beat time, but also used recognisable tempos to signal parades and even meal times in barracks. In 1642 the Royalist commander Thomas Bulkley wrote that: '... our companyes of men are near full... I gave all my Captains leave to be forward before I began presuming upon ye beating of my drummes. I should soon rayse my company.' The men had learned in a short period of basic training to parade on hearing a drum beat for them to assemble. The style of drums evolved to become more sophisticated in their construction and allowed the development of complicated drum beats or tunes to be played in combination with other instruments such as fifes and bagpipes.

Armies taking to the battlefield, varying in size from a few thousand to hundreds of thousands, had to be controlled and orders passed via signals. The manoeuvrability and control of an army is often of more importance than its physical size, as is shown by many famous battles throughout history. For example, the Battle of Gaugemela in October 331 BC pitted Alexander the Great, with fewer than 50,000 men, against Darius III, who led a Persian army of over 100,000 men. Some believe that the Persian army may have been larger, but the eventual outcome was a victory for Alexander after he skilfully manoeuvred his infantry and cavalry. Control over armies of this size would have been very difficult during this period, but not impossible. At the Battle of Breitenfeld in 17 September 1631, during the Thirty Years' War, the opposing sides were considerably smaller than those at Gaugemela, but the armies had marched to the location and in battle they still required signals to be controlled. We learn from accounts that at one point in the battle, artillery exchanged fire for some two hours to the accompaniment of 'trumpets and drums'. The battlefield at Gaugemela is estimated to have been about 1 mile in depth, while at Breitenfeld the battlefield measured about 2.5 miles deep and the drummers had to struggle to make themselves heard above the noise of muskets and artillery.

Over the centuries armies became better trained and drilled, with each unit moving as a single cohesive body, such as the pike blocks of the seventeenth century. An army marching on campaign had to move in an orderly manner so as to remain a single force and arrive at the same time when preparing for battle. For this reason drill had to be rigid and marching formed the basis of this, with instructions to carry weapons and how to move in column. Similarly, in later centuries, as the use of firearms spread, musketeers had to be trained and disciplined through drill to load and fire as one. The historian John Keegan confirms this in his book *The Face of Battle*: '… drill [was], the most important military innovation of the sixteenth century, requiring that a man stay where put instead of wandering about looking for a worthy adversary…' Here was the beginning of steadfastness and military discipline, which would decide the outcome of battle. If troops held firm in battle through the strict discipline instilled by continuous and arduous drill, with men armed with muskets going through the routine in drill book fashion on the battlefield, then they could win the day if they maintained firepower: 'Load–Make Ready–Level (Aim)–Fire'. An example of such steadfastness is shown at the Battle of Fontenoy on 1 May 1745 during the War of Austrian Succession. The opposing lines of French and British musketeers marched ever closer until called to a halt and ordered to prepare to open fire. Protocol and chivalry were traits still being observed on the battlefield at the time and the French officers invited the British to fire first. The British officer, Lord Charles Hay, responded to his opposite number by declining the offer saying, 'No, sir, we never fire first. After you'. As the British ranks braced themselves against the deadly salvo, a Guardsman was heard to mumble, 'For what we are about to receive, may the Lord make us truly thankful'. The French knew the reputation of British firepower and were uneasy about firing first, their aim impaired by the thought of what was to come in the wake of having fired. Once the French had fired their volley the British lines advanced to close the distance to around thirty paces. If we take it that each step was approximately 30in in length the gap between the two sides had been closed to around 75ft. The French were still reloading when the British halted, raised their muskets, took aim and fired. The musket balls ripped into the closely packed ranks, killing and wounding nineteen officers and some 600 other ranks. Thirty years later at the Battle of Bunker Hill on 17 June 1775 in North America, the infantrymen of the defending Continental Army were ordered to hold their fire until '…you see the whites of their eyes'. Such was the discipline instilled in the troops by drill.

In 1607 the Dutch author Jacob de Gheyn's published a book entitled 'Wapenhandlingen van roers, musquetten ende spiessen' ('Arms Drills with Arquebus, Musket and Pike'). Illustrated with detailed drawings by John of Nassau, the book was the first modern drill manual and used pictures to enhance the words and show the various drill movements. This was adapted by other countries and other works also appeared. The role of the drummer in drill parades became apparent when it came to timing to complete a drill move, especially marching. During drill parades, drummers would be present to tap out the timing on their drums so that all the troops moved at the same time and responded to the orders in unison. There were some twenty-four separate movements for loading and firing a musket, and this had to be done as a single unit if a steady rate of firing was to be sustained during battle. Drummers are still used to tap out the time for drill to this day, practicing in readiness for large ceremonial parades such as the Trooping of the Colour in London. A warrant dating from around 1631–1632 was issued in England to specifically cover drum music and also included regulations for drum banners. This document is one of the earliest records directing how drums should be played, what tunes were allowed and how they should be decorated.

The drill manoeuvres we see soldiers performing today at ceremonial parades, such as Bastille Day in France, where a large military march occurs in Paris on 14 July each year, has its origins dating back to the tactics on the battlefield of the eighteenth and nineteenth centuries. Some of these were highly complex, such as the 'Oblique Order' as used by the Prussian army of Frederick the Great. Some believe that this tactic was one of the most important battlefield manoeuvres of the mid-eighteenth century. The execution of the tactic depended on rigid discipline, even under the most difficult of conditions. It was designed as an alternative to attacking the enemy head on and along the entire front. It was a shock tactic designed to catch the enemy off guard and involved advancing in echelon against one of the enemy's flanks to outnumber and overwhelm it before it could be reinforced. It was really quite a simple tactic and involved the Prussian army advancing behind an advance guard, which kept the enemy's attention focussed on them to the front. The following units were then given the signal to form 'oblique order' and move to one of the enemy's flanks and attack from the side. The manoeuvre was screened by the advance guard, which kept firing, and once the flank had started to give way under pressure the Prussian cavalry was sent in.

It was a successful tactic during the eighteenth century and Frederick the Great was recognised as a master tactician, but this had not always been the case. It took time to formulate new tactics and train troops to carry them out, and at the Battle of Mollwitz in 1741 he barely won against a force of equal numbers. During the Seven Years' War (1756–1763), and despite the tactical advantages available to him using the 'oblique order', he is understood to have used it only twice. The first time was at the Battle of Leuthen in 1757 and again the following year at the Battle of Zorndorf in 1758. Prussian army drill was legendary in this period and left a startling impression on those who witnessed the infantry being manoeuvred. During exercises in Silesia in 1785, a column of 23,000 Prussian infantry performed a wheel, with a single cannon shot as the only signal for the manoeuvre to be made. Within seconds and without confusion the column formed into a line some 2.25 miles in length.

Armies had always marched great distances on campaign, but from the eighteenth century it was the speed with which these marches were completed that was most remarkable . Most armies marched at around seventy-five paces per minute, but the French and Prussian armies observed seventy-six paces per minute, which may seem a small increase but is significant when it comes to timing. The length of stride also varied, with the French army having three lengths of stride, the shortest being 12in, then 24in and the more standard 30in. The ordinary speed of seventy-five paces per minute was used when marching, but when contact was made with enemy this would increase to 'double', with anything from 108 to 120 paces per minute. In Saxony around 1789, this double speed or *dublir* pace was up to 140 paces per minute, with a length of stride set at 1 *Elle*, equal to 58.4cm (just under 23in). The Prussians length of stride was 28in, all of which was accompanied by drummers tapping out the pace.

Typically, a French unit of infantry could cover between 10 and 12 miles per day at ordinary marching speed. The column was headed by pioneers, *tete de colonne* (head of column) carrying axes, and behind them marched the drum-major, followed by the drummers and musicians. The British army at around this time would also cover similar distances on the march. By comparison, over 2,000 years earlier, legionaries of the Roman army could march distances of between 18 and 20 miles per day. The Romans had built roads with good surfaces and which were well drained, making marching easier; however, these prepared routes did not extend to all locations and they had to move over unprepared ground at times. Road surfaces in eighteenth- and nineteenth-century Europe were far from being ideal and at times were little more than dirt tracks which were washed away during storms. Some surfaces were cobbled and yet the distances covered on the march still remained at an average of 10 to 12 miles, although there were exceptions with forced marches being completed in record times. All the while the men had to carry all their equipment and weapons, and the drummers marching with the column had to move at the same speed carrying their drums and personal equipment in haversacks on their back.

The basic marching distance covered each day would not have unduly exhausted the men, but if they also had to forage for food then they would have become increasingly tired and struggled to keep to the pace. The time taken to cover the set daily distance could be reduced by 'stepping up the pace' from seventy-five paces per minute to 108 paces per minute, and some quite prodigious achievements in marching were set. In 1796, the same year that Andre Estienne beat his drum so vigorously at Arcola in Italy, Napoleon Bonaparte fought two engagements and a full battle within a week, with Augereau's division and Massen's division marching 114 miles and 100 miles respectively. Later, when Napoleon ordered the Grand Army away from the French coast to join the campaign against the Austrians, the corps under Lannes and Soult covered 152 miles in thirteen days on secondary roads. Davout's corps marched 175 miles in sixteen days with their route taking them over mountainous roads. Soldiers of the day remarked in typical military humour that: 'Our Emperor makes war not with our arms but with our legs'. While such distances sound remarkable, they were actually only covering 10 to 11 miles on average per day. The remarkable thing about such marches is the number of troops involved, and that they arrived as a single force ready to give battle. Davout's corps covered 70 miles in forty-eight hours after a forced march, arriving ready for the Battle of Austerlitz on 2 December 1805. If we assume this was non-stop then the march equates to almost 1.5 miles per hour, which is amazing considering they had artillery and a baggage train. On such marches, soldiers ate, smoked their pipes, sang and talked, and some even became so tired that they slept on the march, moving like automatons. Captain Jean Coignet wrote of a typical march: '... music played, drums beat a charge; nothing got the better of sleep'. The ability to march at speed gave rise to the term 'Steal the march on', which is to arrive unexpectedly and surprise one's enemies before they are ready. This was something Napoleon's armies showed they could do time and again.

THE CORPS OF DRUMS
IS ESTABLISHED

Military forces have enjoyed a long-standing association with music which goes back many centuries. Indeed, it is well documented that armies in ancient Greece and Rome marched into battle to the accompaniment of trumpets and horns. In ancient Egypt the armies of the Pharaohs marched to the sound of horns, cymbals and sometime drums, and it was, therefore, only natural that military forces should maintain this tradition with troops sometimes singing to the most popular tunes. By the beginning of the seventeenth century, many more European countries were incorporating drums and fifes into the ranks of the army, and those which already had units with drums were expanding the numbers of these instruments as their importance became more understood. This now extended from passing signals on the battlefield to keeping the army marching in step and at a steady rhythm. France was one of those countries to be influenced by trends and absorbed drums into the army through contact with Swiss mercenaries, with their drums and fifes employed in French pay. The Swiss Guard which had been formed in 1616 had its own regular corps of drums and it was only natural that over time such a formation should spread to other French regiments.

As armies increased in size and campaigns extended to cover more ground and for longer periods of time, so the function of music to maintain morale became more important. By the sixteenth century the first regular or standing armies were being created in Europe, and also in Russia where Tsar Ivan IV (Ivan the Terrible) established a regular army during his reign from 1547 to 1584. England, however, would not have a professionally trained standing force comparable to the likes of France until the New Model Army was created in 1645, based on the ideas of Oliver Cromwell during the English Civil War. Sweden had a standing army in 1618 at the time of the outbreak of the Thirty Years' War and this establishment served as the template for other European states who based their armies on the 'Swedish model'. Also, by 1617 the first true military academy, the *Schola Militaris*, had been established by John of Nassau in his native Germany.

Later military commanders, such as Maurice de Saxe in the eighteenth century, would continue to advocate the use of music, and drums in particular, to stimulate the troops' morale in battle. This was a tactic he understood well and realised that something as simple as the music of fifes and drums could encourage troops to move forward, rather than follow their basic instinct to move back, away from danger. Drums especially were considered excellent for this and special corps of drums and fifes would come to be established among armies for this very purpose. It was a purely psychological stimulus and it worked in nearly every case. This idea was nothing new, and accounts dating back to the thirteenth and fourteenth centuries in India record that the practice had actually existed some 500 years before the time of Maurice de Saxe. Even during the Crusades, the Ayyubid manual had recommended that music and drums be played during battle to encourage morale among the troops, whilst at the same time undermining the enemy's confidence.

In August 1762 it was suggested to King Louis XV by the Duc de Biron, a lineage of the Baron de Biron which had continued to succeed to the title, that permanent military bands should be established for the French Regiment of Guard. At the time, the regiment already had a group of musicians comprising two bassoons and two horns, along with four *hautbois* (oboes). The Duc de Biron advised the king to increase these to four *hautbois* and four each of the clarinet, horn and bassoon, and were to be paid for either by the colonel of the regiment or by contributions from the officers of the regiment. The idea was adopted and meant that one of the first proper military bands, as opposed to just fifes and drums for marching or signalling, was established in a similar type of formation already serving with the Swiss Guard.

Companies of infantry had had drummers and fife players attached to them since the sixteenth century and it was their role to lead the unit when marching. However, besides this and the role of signalling on the battlefield, the drummer also had other duties accorded to him, one of which was during a parley, where he was expected to walk forward with his commander to discuss terms of conduct on the battlefield, such as agreeing on a surrender or armistice and treatment of the wounded and prisoners. Drummers took their place standing in the ranks of troops on the battlefield, although it was widely understood that they held non-combatant status and that they should not be harmed. This was a great improvement from 300 years earlier when drummers had been deliberately targeted for particular attention and were killed to prevent them from signalling. However, it was inevitable that some drummers would be killed or wounded in the general mêlée of battle. As armies increased in size, so fife players and drummers were organised at battalion level and established as a distinct corps of drums. This tradition is still maintained today and corps of drums are found within regimental formations across Europe and around the world, even in places like South America.

The rank of drummer came to be recognised as an official title of his status and today is still recognised to distinguish him in the same way that private, corporal or musician is used. In charge of the corps of drums was the drum-major, sometimes known as drummer major, and in the case of the British army the corps of drums answers directly to the battalion adjutant. Around 1690 the rank of drum-major-general was created in the English army, as it was known at the time, and this rank was given official status by royal warrant in 1702. However, it was a short-lived title, probably being unique to the English army, and understood to have been abandoned late in the eighteenth century. It was certainly still being used around 1786 when Drum-Major Grose wrote his work 'Military Antiquities' in which he refers to the rank of drum-major-general. According to him the rank was the equivalent to the commission of a subaltern officer and he was placed in charge of granting licences to drummers. It was noted that a drum-major's uniform should, '… never be object [and] that he is too great a coxcomb such an appearance is rather to be encouraged, provided it does not exceed the bounds of proper respect to his superiors: his dress and appointments should all tend to promote that character as it is absolutely necessary for him to strut, and think himself a man of consequence when marching at the head of the Drummers'. The drum-major marched at the head of the corps of drums, carrying the symbol of his rank which was, and still remains to this day, the mace or staff. Drill movements developed over time to govern the movement of the corps of drums, including the direction they were to march and when to stop playing and halt. The creation of the rank of drum-major may have come about as a result of the drummers themselves and the belief in their own superiority. In the work 'The History of Military Music in England', the author by the name of Farmer believed that the first master drummer, called Robert Bruer, was appointed to the rank as early as 1591 and would later become the rank of drum-major.

At the time that Drum-Major Grose was serving in England, his opposite number was serving in France and his career as musician is very different. In 1791 Michel Gesture was listed as a musician in the Paris National Guard at the time when France was being torn apart by the Revolution in 1789. Gesture had joined the Swiss Guard as a musician when he was just 14 years old and would manage to survive the turbulent troubles of the Revolution Wars between 1792 and 1801, going on to serve as bandmaster in the army of the Revolution and continuing this service during the period of Napoleon Bonaparte. He escaped the fury of the 'Revolutionary mob' when they stormed the Tuileries on 10 August 1792 because he was not present at the time of the attack. A group of twelve musicians were lucky to escape death because they were billeted at Courbevoie, but the drummers and fife players of the Royal army were killed by the rioters who overwhelmed the troops by their weight of numbers. Other musicians of the Royal army were far luckier, being spared the same fate when they were imprisoned in the Palais Bourbon and later released when the initial anger of the crowds had abated. When King Louis XVI was being taken to his execution on 20 January 1793, the procession was accompanied by a group of drummers who beat loudly so as to drown out any words of support for the condemned monarch. These drummers would have at one time beaten the signals for the king's army and now they were alerting the crowds that the king was being taken to the guillotine.

In 1754 an order was issued which made it obligatory for all regiments in France to have a corps of drums. The rank or position of drum-major had been established by a similar order in June 1745 and replaced the title of 'chief drummer', which had been established in November 1651. One of the earliest men to be listed in 1769 as a drum-major serving in the French army was called Cholet, whose son was also listed as being a junior drum-major. The rank of drum-major was already in use in the English army in the seventeenth century, which shows that the French were slightly behind in regulating the rank structure among the corps of drums. However, the French would develop a fascination with drums almost to the point of obsession, and over the years the numbers of drums within the ranks of the military would increase so that by 1789 the band of the National Guard, which had been formed that year by Bernard Sarrette, would have the usual numbers of kettledrums and other drums, but these would be joined by up to 300 other drummers for special occasions.

In the seventeenth century we learn that French drum-majors were being paid around the rate of 600 livres (100 years later the rate of pay for the drum-major was around 800 livres, with 1 livre being equal to 1 franc in the old French currency, meaning an annual salary of approximately £3,200 by modern rates). The Swiss Guard also found itself elevated in status when given duties to guard the Louvre, which had at one time been a fortress, as a royal residence and then used to display the French king's art collection in the second half of the seventeenth century. These duties were later extended when the role of the Swiss Guard included protecting the interior of the building. This was a long way from the early days when mercenary troops such as the Swiss had been viewed with suspicion when it came to a loyalty, but were now given a privileged position. The drums in use at this time measured around 42in in height and had a diameter of 37in. The shells of French drums at this time were usually wooden, but some were also beginning to be made from brass sheet and weighed almost 8lbs. An example known to have been captured at the Battle of Blenheim on 13 August 1704 was made from metal and decorated with the French Royal coat of arms and carried the title 'Regiment de Marine'. At this engagement the Allied forces of the Duke of Marlborough and Prince Eugene of Savoy, numbering some 52,000 men, faced a combined Franco-Bavarian force of 56,000 men, commanded by Marshals Tallard and Marsin and the Elector of Bavaria. Drummers and musicians were caught up in the conflagration and one of the popular English tunes at the time was the march known as 'Lillibullero' (subject to many versions over the centuries), which would have been heard as the troops went into battle. Other tunes being composed for specific marches around this time included tempos and drum rolls, such as the one for the Swiss Guard which occasionally marched to the slow rhythm of a composition called '*La Marche de Colin-Tampon*', still in use today with the French Foreign Legion.

The Duke of Marlborough defeated the Franco-Bavarian army, capturing 16,000 prisoners in the process and seizing amounts of equipment, including weaponry and musical instruments. The victory also gave one of the first battle honours in the history of the army to three of the regiments present at the engagement. The first was Douglas's Regiment, which had been raised in 1688 and became known as the 16th Regiment of Foot, before later being known as the Bedfordshire and Hertfordshire Regiment. The second regiment to receive the Blenheim battle honour was Meredith's Regiment, which had been raised in 1702. This regiment would become the 37th Regiment Foot and then the Royal Hampshire Regiment. Last was the Princess Anne of Denmark's Regiment, which had been raised in 1685. This regiment would become the 8th Regiment of Foot and then the King's Regiment (Liverpool). Battle honours are usually embroidered on the Regimental Colours, but some of the more memorable battles are recorded on the drums of the corps of drums and the regimental band, and these take pride of place during parades. Drum-Major Grose records how drums during the reign of King George II (1727–1760) were ordered to be made from wood. Grose does say that metal drums were made, probably copied from designs favoured in either France or the Germanic states. He also mentions that the emblems on the drums, formed from the motifs of the colonels of the different regiments, were to be replaced by the royal coat of arms, along with Regimental Colours and facings.

In his work 'Traite des Armes', published in 1678, author Louis de Gaya describes side drums of the period, which at some point in the seventeenth century were being fitted with a device called a 'snare', a system of fine cords stretched across the lower skin of the drum to increase its resonant sound. Today the snare is made from fine wires and can be adjusted for tension. Gaya describes French drums as: '*Les Tambours sont fait de bois de Chasteigner creux et couverts par les deux costery de peau de veau…*' This tells us the shell of the drum was made from chestnut wood and covered in calfskin. He continues by writing '*… avec un timbre qui est par dessous*'. This description tells us that snares (*timbres*) were fitted under the drum. It has been suggested that the term 'side drum' is derived from the fact that it is carried on the side, which does seem to make sense.

Gaya's book is well illustrated and shows a range of musical instruments, including cornets, fife, *hautbois* and trumpets. He illustrates the *tambour* (drum), but also something he refers to as timbales, which are better known as *nakers* or kettledrums. He explains that they entered Europe through the Balkans and Hungary, and describes them as: '*… deux vaisseaux d'arain, ronds par dessous, don't les ouvertures sont couvertes de peau de Bouc, qu'on fait resoner enbattant dessus avec des baguettes.*' This describes the drum as round vessels covered in goat skin and beaten with sticks. The French apparently did not take to these new forms of

drums immediately and Gaya writes that King Louis XIV ordered them t
used as part of the equipment of the ordanance companies, before which
the French army only used those kettledrums which had been captured in battle.
Kettledrums had been known about earlier and were certainly being recorded
in paintings by artists such as Domenico Ricci, who showed one in his work in
Verona, Italy, around 1530. King Ladislaus of Hungary in 1457 is also recorded as
having drum horses mounting kettledrums for special parades.

Among the other duties assigned to drummers was the designating of billets
to the troops who had to be quartered, and even the delivery of letters and other
written messages. This last duty, because of its importance, would probably have
been performed by the drum-major himself rather than a drummer, even though
his integrity would never be in any doubt. Thomas Simes confirms this when
he noted in 1778 that the drum-major had to '… carry the letters to, and bring
them from the Post Office…' In England during the reign of King William III
(1689–1702), troops could be billeted in inns, barns and stables and '… all houses
selling brandy and strong waters…', although troops could not be billeted in
private dwellings with civilians. Drummers were instructed to sweep and clean
the officers' billets, presumably because of their trustworthiness as opposed to
the ordinary soldier who, despite the consequences, might be tempted to steal
something of value. The combination of troops and alcohol was always going to
be a volatile mixture and knowingly putting troops into establishments which
sold liquor was bound to lead to trouble. The drummer who put troops in such
establishments would be popular, but this would soon disappear when the troops
became drunk and committed crimes, such as theft or even desertion, which
warranted punishment by flogging and had to be administered by the drummer.

Flogging was an unsavoury and unpopular duty for the drummer, but one that
had to be conducted according to military law. Thomas Simes notes in 1778 how
during the convening of a courts martial, a drum-major had to be prepared to
conduct a flogging by having his 'apparatus for punishing…' In an effort to curb
any drunken behaviour which could lead to punishment, some armies began
sending out the drummers to beat a signal to the taverns and inns to stop serving alcohol and for the troops to return to their billets. The Dutch used the term
doe ten tap toe for this signal to tell the innkeepers to turn off the taps of the beer
and wine barrels. Over time this expression became corrupted and anglicised to
'Tattoo', which today has a very different meaning and is used to indicate a ceremonial military parade involving a display by massed bands, such as that held at
Edinburgh in Scotland.

Military justice in all armies was, and still is to this day, dispensed following special tribunal known as a courts martial. Sometimes the singular form of this term
is used as a verb to describe a soldier as having been 'court-martialled for fighting
or theft'. It still denotes that it was a military court which heard the case and passed
sentence in accordance with the military rules and regulations of the country.

In the seventeenth century it was usually the case that officers would convene a form of committee to hear the case against a soldier and then to pass sentence. During the English Civil War, both the Royalist and Parliamentarian armies passed similar sentences on those found guilty of a crime. For example, officers were cashiered, which is to say their services were dispensed with, and blaspheming was punished by having a hole bored through the tongue with a hot iron.

In European armies, and even in England, far harsher sentences could be passed. For example, in the English army the 'Articles of War' first published in 1642 listed twenty-five offences which carried the death penalty, including mutiny, sedition, murder and rape '… whether she belong to the Enemy or not…' By comparison, in 1689 there were more than fifty crimes which carried the death penalty for offenders. The death penalty was also passed on those soldiers who offered violence '… to any who shall bring victuals to the Camp of Garrison, or shall take his Horse or Goods…' For fighting among themselves troops could be sentenced to 'ride the mare'. This punishment was in widespread use and known by various names among the European armies. The prisoner sentenced to this punishment had to sit astride two wooden planks formed together at an angle of around 45 degrees, so that the sharp edge dug into his soft groin area. As if the pain from his own weight was not enough, his agony was added to by having weights, usually service muskets, attached to his ankles to force him down onto the sharp angle of the boards. This punishment could last for several hours and be repeated as many times as judged to be necessary to fit the crime. Drummers would sometimes be required to erect this device and although they were meant to be beyond reproach due to their status, drummers could find themselves subjected to such punishment should they transgress the military code, including being flogged and no doubt also 'riding the wooden mare' which they themselves had built.

In the honours list of unpopularity among officers, the name of Lieutenant-Colonel Jean Martinet, Inspector General of the army of King Louis XIV of France, must be at the top. He was a strict disciplinarian and an ardent believer in drilling the troops so severely that they hated him with a vengeance. The drill and marching would have been completed to the beat of the drum and, although harsh, it did produce results and the troops moved as one, responding to commands without hesitation or question. Martinet established training depots for the troops and his ideas led to mercenaries no longer being required. His name has become synonymous with military discipline and indeed a short-handled 'cat-o'-nine-tails' used to flog as a punishment was named after him. He is known to have been killed in 1672 during an attack at the siege of the city of Duisburg in modern Germany; it is believed he may have been shot by a French infantryman. It will never be known if it was deliberate or accidental, but whatever the case, the sense of relief from his harsh regime would have made the unknown assassin extremely popular with his fellow troops.

Another punishment given for offences such as theft from a comrade was 'Running the Gauntlet'. The guilty party was usually stripped to the waist and had to move along two lines of inward facing troops who were armed with strips of leather or sticks. As the offender proceeded along this human lane he was struck from either side. The punishment dated back to the Roman Empire and was known by various names, such as 'gantlet', a term used by the Continental Army of George Washington during the American War of Independence (1775–1783). Running the gauntlet was also widely used in Sweden and the Germanic states such as Prussia. Death was rare with this punishment, but if a man were sentenced to run the gauntlet a number of times he would often succumb to the beating. Indeed, as one Prussian officer noted that any man sentenced to 'run the gauntlet 36' would usually die from the experience. Whilst drummers may not have necessarily been present during the administration of the punishment of either 'riding the mare' or 'running the gauntlet', they were certainly present at other punishments and were directly involved in their administration.

Flogging was a universal punishment among the armies and some, such as the Prussians and British, were known for their particularly harsh sentences involving flogging. The reputation was not disguised and during the American War of Independence the colonial troops serving in the Continental Army of General George Washington referred to the British troops as either 'lobsters' or 'bloody backs' due to the number of floggings known to be served as punishment. Flogging was widely used as punishment in the British army, but the nickname was not entirely correct because there were some enlightened officers who questioned the efficacy of flogging as a deterrent against committing further misdemeanours. Senior officers such as General Thomas Gage, commander-in-chief in America, interceded in some cases and overturned the sentence of flogging. On one occasion during the war, a British soldier charged with being insolent to an officer was expected to be flogged, but the courts martial dismissed the case. He still expected to be flogged for striking his sergeant, but the man's officer argued that if he was not convicted of the original charge against him, then how could he be flogged for the lesser offence. Other British officers at the time, such as Major-General, The Earl, Hugh Percy and Major-General William Howe, shared the same attitude as General Gage and sentences of floggings were either much reduced or overturned.

The number of lashes given as sentences could run into the thousands. For example, in 1712 a Guardsman killed his colonel's horse and sold the hide. Found guilty of the crime he was sentenced to seven separate floggings each of 1,800 lashes; in total, an unimaginable 12,600 lashes. The man received his first sentence of 1,800 lashes and, unsurprisingly, it almost killed him. On hearing of the incident and the barbarity of the sentence, Queen Anne remitted the remaining 10,800 lashes. George Washington was concerned that if his men stole from the local populace his army would become ostracised and lose support, so any crime of theft was punished severely. The Continental Army did use the death penalty in extreme cases, but largely it too followed the British example of flogging as punishment. Being very religious in his beliefs, the sentence of flogging was passed in accordance with the 'Law of Moses', which meant forty lashes 'save one'. In other words only thirty-nine were given, but on occasion as many as 100 lashes were applied, although the sentence was never on a par with the British punishment which could be 1,000 lashes or as few as twenty-five for minor offences. Washington had to be most careful about sentencing either capital or corporal punishment in a largely volunteer civilian force. If he were to prove too draconian in his harshness, then he stood to alienate further volunteers willing to serve in his Continental Army and so a fine balance had to be established.

Flogging with the device known as the 'cat-o'-nine-tails' was probably introduced sometime in the early part of the eighteenth century. It was made with a wooden handle to which were attached nine lengths of cord, usually knotted, and the name is thought to refer to the resemblance of the tails of a cat. There was no set design for the device and although it could vary in the number of 'tails', the prescribed length of these were usually about 2ft. Certainly in the British army, the 'Articles of War' did not specify the number of lashes which could be applied and it was left to an officer's discretion as to many strokes of the lash should be used. Exactly when and how drummers came to be associated with the administering of corporal punishment is not entirely clear, but it is a task which could not have made them popular with the ordinary soldiers. Drum-majors oversaw the administration of the punishment and some may have instructed the drummers to use both hands. This is very strange because the angle at which a lash is applied does not lend itself to the use of both hands at once. Vertical movement, such as chopping wood, allows both hands to be used to add weight to the task. Movement with both hands in the horizontal plane is not so easy and as the arms extend one will deliver more force than the other. If anything drummers would have alternated hands and probably changed sides depending on the hand being used to apply the lash. Illustrations do exist showing men being flogged by left-handed drummers as well as right-handed drummers. There could be no shirking in their duty and drummers had to 'lay on' the strokes or risk being accused of leniency. Some men would have understood the drummers were only obeying orders or else they too would be flogged for dereliction of duty, but it could not have been an easy task in trying to come to terms with the fact. If it was thought a drummer was not doing his best he would be either kicked or knocked to the ground by the drum-major; a humiliating act, but preferable to being flogged.

This was certainly the case concerning two deserters who were sentenced to flogging in front of their regiment, assembled to witness the punishment at a location in Colnbrook. Two drummers were detailed off too flog each man and once the offenders had been secured to the framework formed by halberds, the signal to begin the punishment was given. The drummers set about their task, but it appears the officer was not satisfied with their efforts. He ordered they be arrested and made it known to the assembled troops that the drummers would face a flogging of 300 lashes the next day for failing in their duties. Four more drummers were ordered forward to replace their disgraced comrades. Removing their tunics they set about their grim task and, not wishing to face the same fate as their comrades, laid into the deserters with heavy hands. Their first strokes raised red wheals on the offenders' backs and when fifty strokes had been reached they were a 'bloody red mush'. On completion of the punishment the men were taken down from their restraints and led away. One 18-year-old soldier by the name of William Lawrence, whose regiment we unfortunately do not know, was sentenced to receive 400 lashes for being absent for twenty-four hours. He later wrote how he '... was lashed [tied] to the halberds. The Colonel gave the order for the drummers to commence. Each drummer gave me 25 lashes in turn.' The army was not entirely without pity, for after administering such fearful punishment the wounds of the flogged men were treated and dressed, and in the case of young Lawrence his punishment appears to have been stopped after 175 lashes because he had pushed the halberds so hard that the drummers had to follow him around the parade ground striking at him. The punishment was probably halted more to prevent embarrassment and the punishment dissolving into farce. In the case of the disgraced drummers who failed in their duty at the Colnbrook punishment, they would have been flogged the following day. Drummers were not immune to punishment and for failing to have their drums with them at all times, errant drummers could expect to receive twenty-five lashes for such dereliction, which in all probability meant a drummer flogging a fellow drummer. Drummers had to carry their drums on campaign the same way that an infantryman had to carry his musket. It was the symbol of his role and had to be kept in good condition, just as an infantryman would maintain his musket.

It is easy to understand why the first set of drummers at the punishment parade at Colnbrook did not strike hard; they wanted to spare the two men, who they probably knew, the pain of being flogged. All they succeeded in doing was prolonging the men's agony and then being sentenced to the same punishment themselves. Captain Thomas Simes, an author of several books on military conduct, reports in 1778 that a man sentenced to receive 100 lashes for his offence should also pay 2d. He remarks that the lash should have no more than 'nine tails' or strings to inflict the flogging. Any man sentenced to be punished by flogging for a second offence would pay 6d (equal to 2.5 pence in modern British currency). If his observations did indeed occur, then this was a case of adding insult to injury and paying for the privilege of being flogged. Drum-Major Grose in 1786 believed that flogging in such a manner had been in use by the army for at least thirty years.

A flogging was usually conducted in front of the assembled ranks of the prisoner's regiment, who were paraded to witness the punishment. The commanding officer witnessed the sentence along with the adjutant and the medical officer.

The drum-major directed the drummers in their duty and on some occasions they would alternate in the flogging after twenty-five strokes so they would not become tired. The prisoner may have a strip of leather inserted into his mouth on which to bite and if he fainted he could be revived by having cold water thrown over him. In 1787 Dr Robert Hamilton was serving as a medical officer with a regiment in the British army and, having witnessed a flogging, he wrote an account in 'The Duties of a Regimental Surgeon Considered', which was published in that year. It is safe to assume that it was drummer administering the punishment which Hamilton observed: 'Hall was sentenced to receive five hundred lashes for house-breaking; he got four hundred of them before he was taken down; and in the space of six weeks was judged able to sustain the remainder of his punishment, as his back was entirely skinned over. The first twenty-five lashes of the second punishment tore the young flesh more than the first four hundred, the blood pouring at the same time in streams. By the time he got seventy-five his back was ten times more cut by the 'cats' than with the former four hundred … it was thought prudent to remit the remaining twenty-five…' This is interesting because the doctor witnessed the sentence and felt appalled by what he saw, and yet it would have been he as medical officer who deemed the man fit enough to receive the second part of his punishment.

When considering flogging as a punishment, there are three versions from witnesses which must be taken in account. First there is the onlooker, such as the commanding officer, the medical officer, as in the case above, or the assembled troops. Then there is the actual man who has been flogged, and although statements from this quarter are rare, they do exist. Lastly there is the drummer who has had to flog the man. A former drummer, whose name and regiment is not recorded, has left a testimony of his feelings on conducting a flogging. His written account notes: 'At the lowest calculation, it was my disgusting duty to flog men at least three times a week. From this painful task there was no possibility of shrinking, without the certainty of a rattan [cane] over my own shoulders from the Drum-Major, or my being sent to the black hole [prison].' The anonymous author continues: 'After a poor fellow had received about one hundred lashes, the blood would pour down in streams.' He is witnessing exactly the same thing that Dr Hamilton noted, as would occur when a man is continually struck with force by a rope across the sensitive area of his back. The drummer continues by concluding that: '… by the time he had received three hundred, I have found my clothes all over blood from the knees to the crown of the head. Horrified by my disgusting appearance, I have, immediately after the parade, run into the barrack room, to escape from the observations of the soldiers, and to rid my clothes and person of my comrade's blood'. It could never have been easy to undertake the duty of flogging a man, but it was not personal and military discipline had to be maintained.

Written accounts by men who have been flogged are unusual, but in 1848 a former trooper by the name of Alexander Somerville of the Royal Scots Greys, a cavalry regiment with a fine and distinguished history, published an account of the flogging he received in a work entitled 'The Autobiography of a Working Man'. Somerville had joined the regiment in 1831 and does not specify the reasons for being flogged. Being a cavalry regiment, a farrier and a trumpeter administered the flogging, but we can identify with the details the same process by which a drummer in an infantry regiment would have administered the punishment. Having been restrained to the wooden framework, he was ready to receive his punishment in front of the regiment. At the time of his punishment, Somerville was only 21 years of age and goes on to write: 'The regimental Sergeant-Major, who stood behind with a book and pencil to count each lash and write its number, gave the command "Farrier Simpson, you will do your duty"...' Simpson took up the cat-o'-nine-tails and Somerville felt '... an astounding sensation between the shoulders, under my neck, which went to my toe nails in one direction, my finger nails in another, and stung me to the heart, as if a knife had gone through my body...' This was only the first stroke, more and worse was to come. On receiving the second stroke Somerville thought: '... the former stroke was sweet and agreeable compared with that one...' It continued for twenty-five strokes, after which Farrier Simpson handed over the cat to a younger trumpeter who had not flogged before. His inexperience, youthfulness and natural reluctance made Somerville's agony much worse as he: '... gave me some dreadful cuts about the ribs, first on one side and then on the other.' This continued for fifty strokes before Simpson took up the punishment again. Somerville believed these: '... strokes were not so sharp as at first; they were like blows of heavy weights, but more painful than the fresh ones... He travelled downwards, and came on heavier than before, but, as I thought, slower. It seemed a weary slowness for the sergeant-major, to be counting the fifteenth and sixteenth of the third twenty-five'. By now seventy-five lashes had been administered and for Somerville it must have felt like an eternity, for he speaks for the only time during the punishment to say: 'Come on quicker, Simpson, and let it be done; you are very slow'. Somerville received the last of the lashes and, when he thought he could not take any more and was about to plead for mercy, the punishment was at an end. It was barbaric, but as a veteran of the Peninsular Wars in Spain wrote of the treatment meted out to soldiers by Major-General Robert 'Black Bob' Craufurd, the commanding officer of the Light Division during the retreat to Corunna in 1808–1809: '... if he flogged two, he saved hundreds from death'. General Craufurd was a strict disciplinarian, much like Lieutenant-Colonel Martinet, and also fell in battle leading a charge during the siege of Ciudad Rodrigo in Portugal on 19 January 1812. However, unlike his French counterpart, Craufurd was not the victim of so-called 'friendly fire' from his own side, but was killed by enemy action. Farrier-Major Wilson said of his role when administering a flogging that he gave '... a fair blow. We flog gentler than any other regiment. In the infantry I have seen men receive half-minute strokes to the roll of a drum. That is much more severe punishment'.

Flogging in peacetime was abolished in the British army in 1868, the same year that public hanging was abolished, but soldiers could be flogged on campaign until 1881. Gradually other armies forbade its use as punishment, thus relieving the drummer of a great and terrible responsibility. If the thought of flogging a man was abhorrent to drummers and drum-majors, then the prospect of capital punishment must have filled them with dread. Execution is the ultimate expression in punishment and the military was no exception if discipline was to be maintained. Execution by either firing squad or hanging was reserved for the most severe of offences, including mutiny and murder. After the controversial execution of Admiral Julian Byng for failing to hold Minorca against the French in 1756, French author Voltaire satirised: '... in this country, it is good to kill, from time to time, an admiral to encourage the others'. His comment may have concerned the unfortunate admiral, but was equally apt for the army and its treatment of soldiers under penalty of death. Hanging could also be reserved for rebels such as Colonel Percy Kirke who, after the Battle of Sedgemore on 6 July 1685 following the failed Monmouth Rebellion, ordered the summary execution of rebel followers of the Duke of Monmouth. They were hanged near the gates of the town of Bridgwater in Somerset and when Colonel Kirke observed the prisoners' feet were twitching in their death throes, an observer noted: '... he [Kirke] would give them music to their dancing, and he immediately commanded the drums to beat and the trumpets to sound'. Harsh treatment indeed, but it was repeated all across the county of Somerset where 'the Hanging Judge' George Jeffreys ordered the execution of more rebels for the 'encouragement of others'. A drummer, Adam Wheeler, served with the Wiltshire Militia in the kcing's army and later wrote of the 500 rebel prisoners taken to the church in the village of Westonzoyland: 'The first number was fifty and five, most of them tied together. The third was two wounded on their legs, crawling upon the ground on their hands and knees to Weston Church.' In total twenty-two rebels were hanged there in a bloody retribution. Today, commemorative plaques can be found across Somerset on buildings where the executions took place in Glastonbury, Shepton Mallet and Somerton.

In 1802, troops were ordered to parade at Portsdown Hill near Hilsea Barracks to witness an execution of a deserter; it is estimated that some 15,000 men paraded to watch this exhibition for the 'encouragement of others'. Deserters were usually flogged for their efforts, but for a man to be sentenced to execution would indicate that he had committed other more serious offences during his period of unlawful absence, or was a serial absentee and of poor standard as a soldier. Whatever the reason, the fact remains that the man in this case was sentenced to be executed by firing squad. The military has traditionally used either firing squad or hanging as the forms of execution, and available troops were assembled to watch the punishment. On the date of the Portsdown Hill execution, a witness, Rifleman Harris of the 95th Regiment of Foot, who was also a member of the firing squad, wrote how the condemned man was quite composed and confessed how it was drink which had brought him to this. Harris states that on being acknowledged by the drum-major of the Hilsea Barracks they loaded their weapons and stood ready. It would appear from this description that no actual words of command were given because Harris continues in his statement that there was: '… then a dreadful pause for a few moments, and the Drum-Major, again looking towards us, gave the signal before agreed upon, and we levelled and fired'. The signal in this case was a movement of either his cane or drum-major's mace, at which point the men fired. Although several bullets had struck the poor man he was apparently still alive. At this point Harris notes how: 'The Drum-Major also observed the movement and, making another signal, four of our party immediately stepped up to the prostrate body, and placing the muzzles of their pieces to the head, fired, and put him out of his misery.' The execution complete, the parade were then ordered to march past in slow time and, on the command, turn their heads to look at the body to emphasise the fact that the military had the power of life and death over each soldier. As long as he obeyed orders and did not commit any offence, he had nothing to fear except, perhaps, being killed in battle. Even so, that was part of his duty and if he ran away in battle, then this act of cowardice would bring about execution. The parade would almost certainly have marched off to the accompaniment of the band or corps of drums, because other witness accounts of executions state the regimental band was present for the men to march. The drummer was involved in all levels of punishment from the most minor infractions which warranted a flogging, through to the ultimate penalty of death.

Courts martial were the official military courts governing the regulations of the army and the navy, and the officers sitting in judgement dispensed the punishments. In time of peace under ordinary circumstances these courts martial were usually convened in barracks; however, in times of war military justice must still be conducted and courts martial convened, and for this reason a special tribunal was established known as 'Drumhead Courts Martial' for the purpose of holding a trial involving crimes committed whilst on campaign. It is believed the term originates from the fact that drums were sometimes used as extemporised tables for use as writing surfaces or desks when campaign orders, messages or official records of proceedings had to be kept. The term has come to be associated with summary justice, when sentences of flogging and hanging were dispensed very quickly, usually whilst on campaign, to complete the trial without delay. One of the earliest written accounts of drumhead courts martial on record appears in the memoirs of Brigadier-General Sir Charles Shaw, who served with Wellington's army during the Peninsular War in Spain and Portugal. Drumhead courts martial were convened to deal with incidents such as the horrific atrocities committed by the Allied army following the fall of the city of Badajoz in Spain, which had been besieged between March and April 1812. When the city was captured the British army in particular went on the rampage, killing and raping civilians. Commanders such as 'Black Bob' Craufurd are known to have ordered drumhead courts martial trials to be convened for the 'encouragement of others'. On one occasion, General Craufurd ordered a drumhead courts martial to try two men who had straggled behind their regiment, passing sentence of 100 lashes each. As sentence was being passed a man was heard to say 'Damn his eyes'; the man was sentenced to receive 300 lashes for his impudence, such was the justice which could be expected at these hearings. However, drumhead courts martial were held long before the Peninsular campaign and the French artist Jacques Callot (1592–1635) included an illustration of such a case in his work of 1633 entitled 'Les Grandes Miseres de la Guerre' (The Great Miseries of the War), which includes eighteen such similar prints. Another illustration in the same work, which shows the hardships and sufferings on campaign, includes punishments such as hangings and shows a drum being used as some form of table under the tree from which the condemned are hanging. It is indeed a grim reminder of the harsh realities of war in the seventeenth century, and that both civil and military justice could be swift and extreme.

The punishment of 'Drumming Out' was the humiliation usually reserved for disgraced soldiers, but was often used for officers who were stripped of their rank and medals in front of the assemblage of the man's regiment and then drummed out of the service as he walked toward the barrack gates. One of the earliest recorded names known to be discharged by drumming out is Lieutenant Frederick Gotthold Ensiln of the Continental Army, who was disgraced for the crime of sodomy during the American War of Independence. He was most fortunate to be given such a lenient sentence, considering that the crime of sodomy in the British Royal Navy at that time was punishable by hanging. Some sources claim the term drumming out was first used ten years before the outbreak of the American War of Independence, when it appeared in the work 'The Life of John Buncle' by Thomas Amory and says '… they ought to be drummed out of society…' This may not be the case, as during the English Civil War five mutinous troopers in the New Model Army in 1649 were told: 'You shall ride with your faces towards the horse tails before the heads of your several regiments, with your faults written on your breasts, and your swords broken over your heads'. Whilst not exactly written down the inference here is that the men were effectively being 'drummed out' with all the ignominy that entailed. The expression 'swords broken over your heads' is more likely to be symbolic because no sword could be broken in such a manner. The blade of the sword is designed to withstand severe force during battle and it is more likely the sword was broken using considerable force and the weapon then dubbed on the man's head in a gesture of the ruling. Mutiny and desertion affected both sides in the English Civil War and discipline had to be enforced and punishments dispensed according to the crime. Hanging was usually passed as sentence for mutiny, but a man could also face a firing squad for this crime. Men sentenced to be drummed out of their regiments probably received the punishment for misdemeanours of a smaller scale and the sentence was more for humiliation and to set an example, without resorting to capital or corporal punishment.

In later centuries, a soldier being drummed out would have badges and buttons ripped off his uniform, along with medals if he had any. The man would then be forced to march through the barracks or garrison behind the drums and then would be physically kicked out of the gates. In some countries, such as England and America, the disgraced soldier would be accompanied by the tune known as the 'Rogues' March', which completed his humiliation and was sometimes referred to as 'John Drum's entertainment'. A soldier on campaign during the Peninsular War later wrote how he was humiliated in the field in this way when the colonel of his regiment ordered: '... the Drum-Major to cut and strip me of all the badges of honour ... and reduced to the rank of private'. The local civilian populace of some garrison towns, such as Windsor in Berkshire, often heard the distinctive sound of drums and assembled outside the barrack gates to boo and heckle the disgraced soldier, adding to his humiliation.

It was not just disgraced officers who could be drummed out of camp or barracks, women of bad reputation, too, could be subjected to the same treatment. Wherever soldiers are to be found so prostitutes will gather to earn money. This has occurred throughout history and the term 'camp followers' was applied to such women, who could prove to be a hindrance to an army on campaign. If women became a nuisance, they had to be physically ejected from the camp and there are instances where they were escorted from the camp accompanied by drummers and officers to see they left the grounds. There are illustrations depicting these scenes, such as one painting dated c.1780 that purports to show a prostitute being drummed out of an army camp in Hyde Park in London. It is quite easy to believe that such occurrences did take place because commanding officers did not want their men to become infected with venereal diseases. In the eighteenth century, however, women were luckier than camp followers of 100 years earlier; during the English Civil War prostitutes were not tolerated and there are accounts of such women having their noses split or their faces marked. So, although drumming out may have been embarrassing, at least it was not life-threatening to the women being conducted from camp.

Despite being connected with administering punishment, drummers still had their non-combatant status and were assigned to act in the role of stretcher-bearers to help carry the wounded from the battlefield to hospital for treatment. In 1906 a standing order issued by the 1st Black Watch stated that: 'As bandsmen are liable to serve in the ranks on any emergency, they are to make themselves thoroughly efficient...' Although this order mentions bandsmen, it would also apply to drummers who would be expected to act as stretcher-bearers in battle. Such duties were universal to drummers, with, for example, drummers of the German army in the First World War serving as stretcher-bearers. Even today, drummers in modern armies around the world still serve in this role. These are humanitarian duties and have no military role except to help save lives. Being non-combatants, the drummers were not supposed to be armed, but traditionally they carried a short sword, which was more for display than an offensive weapon. Modern-day drummers still carry a short-bladed, sword-type bayonet on ceremonial occasions, although, as mentioned, these 'short-swords' would have been more useful as a tool for chopping firewood, cutting bread or other similar tasks rather than being used as an offensive weapon of war. Indeed, in battle a short-bladed weapon would not offer much in the way of defence when attacked by an enemy armed with either a musket or pike, and certainly not against charging cavalry.

Gervase Markham commented on the trumpeter's non-combatant status in his work 'Souldier's Accidence' by writing how he: '...is not bound to any armes at all more than his sword, which in former was not allowed but with the point broken'. This observation tells us that the sword is deliberately blunted by having the tip of the blade removed. From this we can take it that drummers' short-swords would probably have been blunted in a similar manner. Such blunting would certainly render it unfit for any purpose other than as an implement to chop or cut and therefore has to be viewed as a tool in the same way as a butcher's axe or carpenter's hammer. Trumpeters serving with Dragoon regiments in England in the eighteenth century were armed with a pair of pistols carried on the saddle for self-defence, even though they were also considered non-combatant troops.

The dress of the drummer has always been flamboyant and, today, corps of drums around the world still wear very elaborate uniforms. These are usually worn on ceremonial duties, such as the British Trooping of the Colour and Changing the Guard, which is performed at Buckingham Palace and St James's Palace in London and Windsor Castle in Berkshire. The drummers of the five Foot Guards Regiments: Grenadier, Coldstream, Scots, Irish and Welsh, are particularly smart, with the troops wearing scarlet tunics and a distinctive bearskin cap. The tunics of the Guards regiments are laced in a design referred to as 'Christmas tree' pattern, which is white braiding decorated with the *Fleur de Lys* sewn along the seams of their tunics. Drummers in other regiments also have lace braiding sewn along the seams of their ceremonial parade tunics and this is known as 'crown-and-inch' and is attached to the sleeves, collars and even extends down the seams of the back of the tunic.

Even before the outbreak of the Napoleonic Wars (1800–1815), uniforms of the armies across Europe were becoming ever-more flamboyant in style and colour. However, this fashion would reach its height after 1799 when Napoleon was established as dictator of France and First Consul by a *coup d'etat*. The already flamboyant style of drummers' uniforms would flourish in armies across Europe and Britain, and even today some regiments still retain these styles for ceremonial parades, such as the Foot Guards in Britain with their distinctive scarlet tunics.

The drummers in the Bavarian army from around 1789 wore tunics edged with blue and silver lace, while the drummers serving in the forces of the Kingdom of Naples wore tunics of carmine (crimson) colour with white lace edging, and the shoulder epaulets extended to a device known as 'swallows nests' from the resemblance to a bird's nest. Their brass drums would also be decorated in carmine colour and have white 'dog-toothed' hoops. Drummers from the Duchy of Nassau wore tunics edged with yellow and black, with swallows nests on their shoulders and the brass drums were also decorated red and blue. Drummers from the Kingdom of the Netherlands in 1814 wore yellow lace and Portuguese drummers had lace in divisional colours and wore trousers of either dark blue or white with black gaiters.

Prussians drummers also had swallows nests on their tunics and *shako* headdress with a red plume, and drummers serving with Russian Lifeguard 'Jager' Regiments had lace collars and cuffs, and their top hat-style headdress carried a 'pom-pom' coloured orange, white and black. Drummers from Saxony had red plumes and had white swallows nests edged in either green, yellow or black, and drummers in the Swedish army also stood out with plenty of lace attached to the sleeves of their tunics. The Duchy of Wurttemberg wore red plumes and their tunics were highly decorated with lace and swallows nests, with brass drums painted yellow and black. These men wanted to stand out and they succeeded. Line infantry of Napoleon's armies had drummers wearing tunics edged with gold, while some units added further embellishments. Kettledrummers serving with cavalry regiments wore 'Mameluke style' uniforms from the Egyptian campaign, with white feathers and gold braid on a fez or turban, a red waistcoat and light blue shirt edged with gold braid, a blue waist sash and white breeches. The drums themselves were decorated with dark green banners trimmed with gold and embellished with crowned imperial eagles. The horses were also splendidly attired in red colours with ceremonial Turkish harnesses.

A drum design known as the *naker*, which would evolve into the kettledrum had been recorded for some time before making its appearance in European armies. These would increase in size and become popular with cavalry units, who mounted special frames, fitted to large horses and were accompanied by other mounted musicians. In his work of 1682, 'Pallas Armata', Sir James Turner writes: 'There is another martial instrument with the Cavalry which they call the Kettledrum, there be two of them which hang before the Drummers saddle on both of which he beats. They are not ordinary. Princes, Dukes Earls, Generals and Lieutenant-Generals may have them with the troops which are not ordinarily called Life Guards'. During the Jacobite Rebellion of 1715, the regiment of Evans's Dragoons is recorded as parading in Stirling in Scotland with: '... six drummers, Mores with bres drums and the hobys; they roade upon gray horses...' The 'Mores' were certainly Moors from North Africa or Turkey because across Europe at this time many black recruits were to be found in various regiments serving in the corps of drums or regimental band. The 'bres drums' and 'hobys' were brass drums and *hautbois* or oboes, and the 'Mores' were described as riding grey horses. In 1759, Admiral Boscawen brought at least ten 'coloured boys' as a present to his brother, the colonel of Farrington's regiment which had been raised in 1694 when the island of Guadeloupe had been captured, thinking that they:'… prove very ornamental as drummers…' The regiment would later become the 29th Regiment of Foot before becoming the Worcestershire Regiment. By the 1760s, the 29th Regiment was widely renowned for the high standards of its corps of drums, which was composed almost entirely of black troops, some of whom were runaway slaves from the American colonies such as Boston.

These historical references to 'coloured men', 'coloured boys' or 'negroes' are not acceptable in society today, but in this instance we have to remember that such remarks were in common usage during the eighteenth century, as evidenced from the archive records of the day. Records held by the Regimental Museum of the Worcestershire Regiment reveal that for more than eighty years there was a 'Black Corps or Drums' and these documents show that some black drummers served terms of twenty and even more than thirty years enlistment with the regiment, and were equal in pay, medals and pensions to the white troops. In 1821, as commander-in-chief of the British army, the Duke of York authorised that 'coloured men… [be] … enlisted for the Band…' where they were employed as drummers. Although some were pressed into service, their standard of living was almost certainly better than the lot of their countrymen, who were forced toil in the sugar plantations in the West Indies. Works by artists such as Rembrandt sketched 'coloured men' mounted on horses and playing kettledrums to support the fact that such men were serving in this role during the seventeenth century. The drums are decorated with banners and show what was in fashion following a French warrant from 1631-1632 , which states that kettledrum banners should be decorated in the colour of the regiment and emblazoned with the regimental badge with a depth of 3ft 6in and have a length of 4ft 8in, excluding the fringe.

Permission for Colonel Boscawen to retain the ten black drummers on strength was granted by King George II in 1759. Black drummers would remain an identifiable and integral part of the regiment, even when it became known as the 29th Regiment of Foot, and the custom would last until 1843 when it was finally ended. Records concerning the 29th Regiment of Foot show that one black drummer was discharged from service in 1780 and another ten years later, both of whom received a pension, which was more than their counterparts working as field slaves could ever hope to expect. This would indicate that these men may have been in service as drummers before 1759, but not necessarily with the regiment. Their departure still left eight black drummers and when the regiment sailed from Ireland in 1765 for service in Canada, each company had one black drummer.

In 1768 the regiment was ordered from Halifax, Nova Scotia to Boston. The sight of black drummers in a regiment of the British army inspired great curiosity among the white Bostonians, many of whom were slave owners, and for them to see black drummers mingling with white troops without any apparent animosity must have seemed anathema to the orderly minds of these citizens. Their senses were further outraged when they discovered that these same black drummers would administer floggings on the white troops as punishment for a range of misdemeanours, such as theft and desertion. The local newspaper, *The Boston Evening Post*, on 6 October 1768 carried in its pages the editorial remarks that in its opinion: 'To behold Britons being scourged by Negro drummers was a new and very disagreeable spectacle'. It is unlikely that military floggings would have been witnessed by civilians, as most such punishments were conducted on the regimental parade ground in front of the assembled regiment. It is possible, of course, that rumours were circulated and this led to the account being published on hearsay evidence. How the news of the black drummers flogging white troops came to be made known to the newspaper is uncertain, but it is highly unlikely that it was through the journalist directly witnessing the event.

On 5 March 1770, a unit of the regiment was turned out to deal with a small group of protesting Boston civilians, with orders to disperse them. Sentiments were running high and there was much tension. The small detachment opened fire on the gathered group of civilians, wounding a number and killing four. An investigation into the events surrounding the shooting exonerated Captain Preston, who was serving with the detachment, and six soldiers were acquitted of any charge. However, two men from the detachment were found guilty of the charges and they were sentenced to be branded. It is quite possible that as drummers were used to administer punishment, the black drummers may have branded these men. In 1773 the regiment returned to England and were posted to Dover in Kent. The following year the regiment was inspected and the records of 1774 say that ten black drummers were present and at least three of these were from the original number presented to Colonel Boscawen by his brother, Admiral Lord Boscawen, in 1759, meaning that these men had already completed fifteen years active service with the regiment.

Another review the regiment paraded for was held in Windsor in 1791 and the 29th Regiment of Foot had its black drummers in the ranks, as noted in a record which stated that: 'The drummers, black, beat and play well'. Black drummers continued to serve with the 29th Regiment, even when it was sent to the island of Grenada in the Caribbean Sea. The uniform of the black drummers included a black bearskin mitre-type cap, with a small drum badge at the rear to denote drummer status. Their tunics were yellow with red facings and had intricate lace pattern around the button holes and up the sleeves, completed with swallow nests on the shoulders. At other times the black drummers are shown wearing turbans, with crescent badges or busby-type caps and red plumes, carrying hanger-type swords as side arms. These bladed weapons were more ceremonial than functional and could not be considered as offensive weapons in the true sense of the term.

Whatever period or style of uniform the drummers wore, they would certainly have looked splendid in review order and stood out from the rest of the regiment in the red tunics of the infantry. In 1802 the regiment was once again in Halifax, Nova Scotia and over several years more black drummers joined the ranks. In 1807 the 29th Regiment returned to England and was posted to Deal in Kent where an observer wrote how the: '… Corps of black drummers cut a fierce and remarkable appearance while hammering away on their brass drums'. The following year the regiment was sent to fight in the Peninsular War where it gained the battle honours of Corunna, Talavera, Albuera and Salamanca, along with several other major battles, the names of which could be added to the list of battle honours applied to the drums. Two black drummers died in service in the Peninsular War and three others survived to be awarded the General Service Medal when it was instituted in 1848, more than forty years after their service in the campaign.

After the end of the Napoleonic Wars in 1815, the numbers of black drummers serving with the 29th Regiment gradually declined and a report records that there were only four '… men of colour…' Eight years later in 1829, a record tells how during that year the regiment had '… three black musicians, the remnants of a Corps of black drummers, two of whom had been 27 years in the Corps'. By 1833 there were only two black drummers remaining with the 29th Regiment. The last serving drummer, George Carville, died of cholera whilst in service in India in 1843, thereby bringing to an end an unique era for the 29th Regiment of Foot and the British army. When Carville died, he bequeathed the sum of £5 to his next of kin, named in his will as being Private Joseph Prindale of the same regiment. The fact that Prindale was white is a testimony to how well black and white troops got on together in the regiment.

The Museum of the Worcestershire Regiment (of the 29th Regiment of Foot, the Worcestershire Regiment) has compiled a comprehensive list of forty-five names of known black drummers who served with the regiment. A study of this list is most revealing and shows a wealth of detail concerning the service of these men. For example, John Charloe is recorded as being born on the island of St Kitts in 1719 and enlisted in the British army in 1751, making him 32 years old in a time when the average life expectancy was between 35 and 37 years old. He is recorded as serving as a drummer and was discharged with a pension in 1780, aged around 61 years old, having completed twenty-nine years of service. Drummer John Bacchus tells a similar story, born on Jamaica in 1726 and enlisting in 1752 aged around 26 years old, he is listed as a drummer in 1774 and would almost certainly have known Charloe. Bacchus was discharged after twenty-eight years of service and granted a pension. Joseph Provence was born on the island of St Domingo and enlisted in 1755, being eventually discharged with a pension in 1790 after serving for thirty-five years. These men and others, such as John Jubo who was born in 'Africa', were almost all from slave backgrounds in the West Indies, which included the islands of Antigua, Barbados and Dominica where the sugar plantations were located.

The following list was very kindly supplied by the Worcestershire Regimental Museum and is reproduced with full permission. It is believed that this is the first time the complete list has been published in a work of this nature. The regimental museum believes that there may have actually been as many as fifty black drummers in the regiment at one time. It will be seen that there is also a number of surnames which have been repeated. Again the museum believes this is due to the number of children 'born in the regiment' and they followed their fathers into the ranks and served as drummers. For example, John Bacchus is known to be dead in 1796 from regimental lists, but later a Thomas Othello (Junior) is mentioned and he is thought to have been an under-age drummer who went missing from the muster rolls at the same time as Thomas Othello. This is but one instance and others may yet be revealed in due course. Although drummers, they would have been trained in the use of muskets in case they were called on to serve as infantrymen in an emergency and some might have done.

JOHN CHARLOE: Born St Kitts 1719. Enlisted *c.*1751. Listed serving as Drummer 1765–1774. Discharged with a pension in 1780 after twenty-nine years of service. Name also spelt Charlow.

JOHN BACCHUS: Born Jamaica 1726. Enlisted *c.*1752. Listed serving as Drummer 1774. Discharged with pension in 1780 after twenty-eight years of service. Probably a different John Bacchus was listed as dead in 1796, presumably still serving at time of death.

JOSEPH PROVENCE: Born St Domingo. Enlisted *c.*1755. Listed serving as Drummer 1765, 1774–1791. Discharged with pension 1790, aged 50, after thirty-five years of service.

JOHN BLENHEIM: Listed serving as Drummer 1765.

LUSHINGTON BARRETT: Listed serving as Drummer 1765 and 1774. Died 1787. Noted as dead in 1788.

JOHN ARCHER: Listed serving as Drummer 1765, 1774 and 1791. Present at the 'Glorious 1 June' 1794.

WILLIAM ARCHER: Listed serving as Drummer 1774 and 1791. Reported dead in 1797.

JAMES ARCHER: Listed serving as Drummer 1791. Transferred 10th Light Dragoons 1793. Still serving in 1806.

SAMUEL WALKER: Reported dead 1781.

THOMAS WALKER: Listed serving as Drummer 1765 and 1774. Possibly known as Samuel Walker (above). Served as a Drummer in Captain Thomas Preston's Company during the Boston Massacre of 1770. Noted as deceased in 1781.

THOMAS OTHELLO: Listed serving as Drummer 1765 and 1774. Confirmed drowned 1777.

JOHN RUFAEL: Listed serving as Drummer 1765. Deserted 1770.

ROBERT BAIRD: Born Jamaica 1738. Enlisted 1766. Discharged with pension 1792, aged 54, after twenty-six years of service.

JOHN MACNELL: Born Antigua 1744. Enlisted 1756, aged 12. Listed serving as Drummer 1774. Name also spelt MacNeil or McNeil. Discharged in 1777, aged 33, after twenty-one years of service.

JOHN JUBO: Born in Africa. Enlisted c.1776 Discharged with pension as lame in 1782, aged 21, after six years of service.

WALTER OTHELLO: Listed serving as Drummer 1784. Discharged 1796.

JOSEPH OTHELLO: Listed serving as Drummer 1785.

HUGH BACCHUS: Born 1774. Enlisted 1785 under age; man's service 1792. Transferred to 98th Foot in 1807.

THOMAS BOHANNON: Born Madras, India 1770. Enlisted 1788, aged 18. Discharged with pension 1816. Military General Service Medal with clasps; Vimiera, Talavera, Albuera. Died 1862. Name also spelt Bobannon.

THOMAS RETFORD: Listed serving as Drummer 1791.

JOHN LLOYD: Listed serving as Drummer 1791. Present at the 'Glorious 1 June' 1794.

THOMAS MURPHY: Listed serving as Drummer 1791.

JOSEPH WRIGHT: Listed serving as Drummer 1791. Present at the 'Glorious 1 June' 1794. Transferred to the Royal Newfoundland Regiment 1807.

ISAAC DREW: Listed serving as Drummer 1791. Reported dead 1795.

HENRY GREENBANK: Transferred to 4th West India Regt 1796.

JOHN BAPTIST: Present at the 'Glorious 1 June' 1794. Transferred to 4th West India Regiment 1796.

JOHN DOUGLAS: Transferred to 4th West India Regiment 1796.

JOHN LEWIS: Present at the 'Glorious 1 June' 1794. Transferred to 5th West India Regiment 1796.

PETER MACAY: Present at the 'Glorious 1 June' 1794. Transferred to 5th West India Regiment 1796.

RICHARD SMALL: Transferred to 5th West India Regiment 1796.

THOMAS CAREY: Listed serving as Drummer 1791.

ROBERT GLOVER: Born Antigua. Enlisted 1793. Died in North America 1814.

JOHN SAMPSON: Born Barbados 1782. Enlisted 1798. Murdered in Aberdeen, Scotland 1807 whilst on recruiting tour.

JAMES STARLING: Born Dominica 1784. Enlisted 1798. Died 1811 in the Peninsular campaign.

JOHN DAINE: Born Nevis. Enlisted 1799. Died 1811 in the Peninsular campaign. Name also spelt Deane or Dames.

JOHN FREEMAN: Born Antigua 1783. Enlisted 1800. Discharged with pension 1818. Military General Service Medal with clasps; Roliça, Vimiera, Talavera, Albuera.

PETER ASKINS: Born St Domingo 1791. Enlisted in Berkshire 1800. Discharged at own request 1831. Military General Service Medal with clasps; Roliça, Vimiera, Talavera, Buscao, Albuera. Drew pension in the Mauritius. Died in 1854.

JAMES KEARNEY: Born Cape Breton, Nova Scotia 1787. Enlisted 1805. Discharged with pension 1824.

JAMES PATISON: Born Halifax, Nova Scotia 1791. Enlisted 1805.

GEORGE WISE: Born Halifax, Nova Scotia 1791. Enlisted 1805. Served in Peninsula campaign (Roliça, Vimiera, Talavera, Albuera). Served in Gibraltar and in the war against United States 1814. Discharged with pension 1835. Possibly died before 1848 when General Service Medal was instituted.

ANTHONY GIBSON: Born Jamaica 1795. Enlisted 1815 Ireland. Discharged in Dublin 1818 on reduction in establishment.

BENJAMIN JUMONT: Born Pennsylvania 1793. Enlisted Waterford, Ireland 1815. Died Sabah 1823.

DONALD MORRISON: Born Ponticherry, India 1797. Transferred from 22nd Foot in St Helena 1819. Discharged with pension, Bombay 1827.

GEORGE CARVILLE: Born Limerick, Ireland 1805. Enlisted 1823. Died India 1843, the last black drummer.

HENRY TITE: Born Waterford, Ireland 1804. Enlisted 1825. Discharged with pension, Chatham 1830.

The fate of John Sampson is a rather unfortunate case given that, for the most part, the black drummers and their white comrades in arms served together quite well without any problems. However, to discover that he is listed as being murdered is extraordinary. It appeared that he was killed during a fight with soldiers from another regiment outside a brothel. An account of the incident was published in the *Aberdeen Journal* on Wednesday 9 September 1807, which reported that: 'On the night of Thursday last, a dreadful affray took place at a house of bad fame near the Justice Port, between a party of military, and a black drummer of the 29th regiment, on the recruiting service here, in which the latter was cruelly murdered. The body which bore marks of great violence, was soon after found in the street...' It was a sensation to say the least and stunned the local civilian populace. The newspaper account went on: '...the head and face were dreadfully cut, and the scull [sic] nearly perforated in two places; but the mortal wound was inflicted on the back, through which a bayonet apparently, or other sharp-pointed instrument, had been driven with such violence as the reach the heart...' It was a sad and rather sordid end to a man's life after several years service. The culprit was never caught, but had he been apprehended he would certainly have been hanged for his crime. Whether the attack was racially motivated or incited through alcohol is not known, but it appears to be the only time that violence was levelled against the black drummers by other British soldiers.

The fact that many of these drummers lived into advanced age beyond the average life expectancy at the time is evidence that they enjoyed a better standard of living conditions, including pensions, than those suffered by slaves on the plantations. These men all had names given to them by either the slave families who had once owned them or by the soldiers with whom they served. If this was the only real ignominy they had to endure then they were extremely well off. For example, John Jubo served only six years with the regiment and yet he was discharged with a pension on being diagnosed as being 'lame' and presumably therefore unable to march. He was only 21 years of age and his future prospect was much better than that of a field slave diagnosed with the same condition, who would have been considered worthless and whose future would have been uncertain. John Jubo on the other hand, whilst not exactly 'set for life', would have been quite comfortably off financially with his small pension to augment any salary he may earn in other employment. These black drummers may have been restricted in the level of rank they could attain, but they can be seen as the first ground-breakers against racial intolerance during the height of the slave trade and over a century before the introduction of the Race Relations Act passed in Britain in 1965, which was later to be amended and strengthened. There is no doubt that these men set examples for future black troops, including the black troops who served as drummers in the Union Army during the American Civil War, and were almost 200 years before activists such as Martin Luther King and Malcolm X. There were black soldiers serving in other regiments of the British army at this time, such as Estiphania Pappin from St Domingo, who would rise to the rank of corporal in 1828 after he had joined the 39th Regiment of Foot (later to become the Devon and Dorset Regiment) and served throughout the Napoleonic Wars. Others, such as Edward Bennaway who joined the 2nd Life Guards in 1812, John Monatt from Grenada who enlisted with the 5th Dragoon Guards and served with the regiment until 1825, and Gibeon Lippet who served as a drummer for a short period in the 43rd Regiment of Foot (later to become the Oxfordshire and Buckinghamshire Light Infantry) until he was old enough to serve as an infantryman, before going on to see extensive service during his time spent with the regiment between 1796 and 1826. In 1840, Sergeant-Major George Loy Smith, serving with E Troop of the 11th Hussars in 1840, recorded how '...only three black men [remain] in the regiment: viz Trumpter Murray, Roderick the cymbal player and McKinley the big drummer'. His words appear to express a sadness that these men would not appear to be replaced. Of all the black musicians who served in the British army, it was the black drummers of the 29th Regiment who remain outstanding in their service.

Horses used for the purpose of carrying kettledrums would have been introduced to the drums by being slowly exposed to the noise to prevent them from being startled at the sound. Gradually the horse would have become used to the pounding. However, kettledrums or *nakers* were not always carried by horses and on certain occasions the smaller versions of theses drums were carried on the

back of a man, with another marching behind him to play the drums. This form
of kettledrum is shown in illustrations depicting the Coronation Process of King
James II of England in 1685, and also in a work by Jean Pine dated from around
1730 and showing the Ceremony of the Order of the Bath. On the other side of
the world, Japanese paintings from sixteenth century show similar illustrations of
how the military carried drums into battle during the time of Oda Nobunaga
and Tokugawa Ieyasu. *Nakers* were still being carried in this fashion by drummers
of the Household Cavalry marching on foot at the coronation of Queen Victoria
in 1837. The infantry retained a form of kettledrum or *naker*, but only as a single
drum carried on the chest of a drummer and termed a bass drum. Today this large
instrument is usually with the regimental band as opposed to the corps of drums,
and although it has various dimensions it usually measures between 28in and 30in
in diameter and 12in to 16in deep. Queen Victoria was quite fond of military
music and on one occasion during a performance at Windsor she enquired of the
title of the piece of music being played. The messenger returned with the information that it was called 'Come Where the Booze is Cheap'.

Now that the cavalry had its musicians and drummers, it was only a question
of time before the artillery wanted its own corps of drums. In England these
drums were mounted on wheeled carriages and drawn by four horses, and one
of the first such arrangements appeared in 1689. Drum carriages such as these
were attached to the Duke of Marlborough's artillery train, which at one point
on campaign during the War of the Spanish Succession in 1708, the year of the
Battle of Oudenarde, was recorded as containing eighteen heavy guns, twenty
siege mortars, 3,000 wagons and required 13,000 horses to move it, taking up
some 30 miles of road. The Allied army of over 70,000 men under Marlborough
completed a forced route march from Lessines to Oudenarde, covering the distance of 28 miles in twenty-two hours. The route included crossing the Scheldt
on 11 July, the day of the battle of Oudenarde, and prompted Marshal Vendome
to say: 'If they are there, the Devil must have carried them – such marching is
impossible'. Kettledrums mounted on carriages are later recorded in a regimental
order of 1747, which directs that a drummer '… mount the kettledrum carriage
every night half an hour before sunset to beat till gun firing'. For this task the
carriage was equipped with a seat for the comfort of the drummer. The French
were so impressed by the vehicle that it was copied by them and used by their
own drummers, proving conclusively that imitation is the sincerest form of flattery. Drums were now completely absorbed into every branch of the armies of
Europe, and beyond. As wars continued between European nations, each would
expand its national army and create new regiments. All through this they would
still attire the band and drummers of these regiments in very elaborate uniforms
to continue the tradition from many centuries before. Kings and emperors took
a keen interest in their armies and none more so than Tsar Peter the Great of
Russia, who ruled from 1682 to 1725.

Born in 1672, Peter was interested in all things military from a very early age and on succeeding to the throne he had the entire resources of the country's military at his disposal. For a young boy this was the ultimate in playthings, at a time when most, less fortunate boys his age may have been at sea or working on a farm. Uniforms of western European influence were adopted, but although the ruler of a vast country, Peter did not assume high rank and chose instead to serve in the Preobrazhensky Regiment as a drummer boy where he could indulge his whims by beating the drum. He relished the lowly rank because he believed that in time of peace drummers and artillerymen had more fun and 'made more noise than majors or colonels'. He travelled widely across Europe and even visited England, where he was introduced to King William III. In 1700, aged only 18, he went to war with Sweden where he lost the initial engagement at the Battle of Narva. Learning lessons from this, he reformed the Russian army and returned to the fray which would become known as the Great Northern War. Following a series of further defeats, Peter's army finally beat the Swedes at the Battle of Poltava on 27 June 1709. The war dragged on for twelve more years, before finally ending with the Treaty of Nystad in 1721. Although Peter had modernised his army and built up a powerful navy, the price was costly. When Peter died in 1725, he left behind a legacy which included a standing army of 130,000 men and a navy so powerful it caused concern in Britain.

The Eighteenth Century

The eighteenth century started in much the same way that the seventeenth century had started, which is to say that the continent of Europe was once again embroiled in wars between various nations, emerging or vying for dominance over a region. To meet this expansion in warfare, armies had grown in size, tactics had been developed to meet different situations on the battlefield and new weaponry had been introduced, such as the famous so-called 'leather gun' used by Swedish artillery. Indeed, it was Sweden which made the opening move at the beginning of the century by engaging in the conflict known as the Great Northern War, which started in 1700. It eventually involved Russia and several other northern states and continued until 1721. Thus a serving soldier or drummer could spend his entire army service on campaign in this one war, which was really a series of battles interspersed with periods of calm, much the same as other conflicts of the period. One such example is the War of the Spanish Succession, which broke out in 1701. This war lasted until 1714 and involved Britain, the Netherlands, France and Spain. The conflict would see great battles being fought at Blenheim (2 August 1704), Ramillies (12 May 1706) and Malplaquet (11 September 1709). A number of present-day regiments in the British army have these battles emblazoned on their drums as battle honours, such as the Royal

Lincolnshire Regiment which fought at all the engagements and was known as Grenville's Regiment and then the 10th Regiment of Foot. Another reputation forged during this time was Frederick the Great of Prussia, who enjoyed martial music and may even have composed marching tunes for his drummers to play as his troops campaigned during the War of Austrian Succession. He also devised the 'oblique order' to engage an enemy line from a different direction and this would influence later military commanders such as Napoleon Bonaparte.

Other wars of the period included the Quadruple Alliance (1718–1720), Polish Succession (1733–1738), Austro-Turkish War (1736–1739), Jacobite Rebellion in Scotland (1745–1746), the Seven Years' War (1756–1763) and many others such as the Anglo-Dutch War (1780–1784) which punctuated the century. Armies had not only become larger and more powerful, with better weapons and tactics, they were now being sent overseas to secure territories for countries seeking to expand their national influence and take advantage of the wealth these new lands offered. The eighteenth century was to become a time when military reputations would be made; men such as John Churchill, the Duke of Marlborough, who led the British army to so many victories during the War of Spanish Succession, adding numerous battle honours to the regimental drums, and whose drum carriage had so impressed the French they had copied its style. It was also a time when nations and great empires were being forged. It is true to say that the eighteenth century was a time of great change, but the greatest of these would happen thousands of miles away from Europe on the other side of the Atlantic. Armies had to expand to meet the exigencies of war and all across Europe the drummers beat out the call to attract new recruits to serve with the Colours, and for king and country.

These wars were the largest conflicts of the period, but there were many other smaller and localised wars being fought in other parts of the world. Several European countries, with the most prominent being Britain, France, Spain and the Netherlands, spread out to take advantage of resources in foreign lands to control trade routes and establish empires. Sometimes these nations came into conflict, such as Britain and France which clashed over Canada and on the Indian sub-continent, where they conducted the fighting in typical European style with massed ranks of troops wearing brightly coloured uniforms and arrayed in ranks interspersed with drummers. India was already a highly civilised nation long before Europeans entered the continent and had its own method of conducting war. However, that did not prevent European states from exporting their own methods of militarism, which eventually took over. The same happened on the other side of the world on the North American continent.

In North America, Britain and France were in open conflict, which spread out across the endless territory and had spilled further north into Canada by the 1750s. This resulted in several hard-fought campaigns, but none more so than the audacious attack conceived by the British in 1759. In a daring operation, a British force led by Major-General James Wolfe sailed up the St Lawrence River and climbed the steep rock faces to reach the Plains of Abraham to attack the French town of Quebec, defended by a strong garrison under the Marquis de Montcalm. The British carried everything with them for the ensuing battle, dragging all their equipment up the steep incline, including at least one piece of artillery, and the drummers struggled over the terrain with their drums. On reaching the summit, the British moved out to take position ready to give battle in the European style, with massed ranks of infantry in line with drummers interspersed. The French moved out to meet them and the battle developed into a typical European clash. During the fighting Wolfe was killed and Montcalm mortally wounded, but the British had carried the day. The French garrison surrendered on 18 September 1759 and was allowed to march out of the town with full military honours, including flags flying and drums playing. Two years earlier the French had allowed the British garrison to leave Fort William Henry with similar honours, but as the column was making its way out of the area, it was attacked by native Indians fighting for the French and many were killed. The surrendering French leaving Quebec had no need to fear such treatment. One of the regiments fighting at Quebec was Mordaunt's Regiment, which called itself 'Wolfe's Own' in commemoration of the battle. The battle honour was conferred on the regiment, which later became the 47th Regiment of Foot and then the Loyal Regiment (North Lancashire), with the regimental drums painted with the honour 'Quebec 1759'. A regimental return for those killed, wounded and missing in the battle shows that four drummers were wounded in the fighting. One was wounded in the unit commanded by Brigadier-General Robert Monckton; one was wounded in the unit commanded by Lieutenant-General Phillip Bragger and two more were wounded whilst serving under Lieutenant-General Peregrine Lascelles of the 47th Regiment of Foot. Such records, again, show that although of non-combatant status, drummers were counted among the casualties on the battlefield. By April 1760, the French had surrendered the whole of Canada and Britain now had colonies stretching across America and up into Canada, reaping the trading benefits which came with such territories.

British soldiers had to be posted to these frontier garrisons to protect these newly conquered lands and they behaved as they would have done on campaign in Europe or when billeted in England. This meant a routine of building roads, constructing barracks, drill and the attendant punishment parades for desertion and other crimes. However, not all was well and there was unrest among the civil population. America at that time was divided into thirteen colonies and governed from Britain, which ordered the raising of taxes and the passing of Acts of Law. This was not popular with the civilian colonists, who grew evermore disaffected at the state of things and rumours of revolution emerged. The countdown to war came on 18 April 1775 when the British army marched to seize weapons and other arms from the colonists at Concord. A mounted messenger had forewarned the colonists to expect military intervention and they readied themselves. No one knows who fired that fateful shot into the crowd of around seventy men gathered on the Lexington Common on 19 April, but it was the '… shot heard "round the world"'. Further firing by British troops left eight men dead and ten wounded. After they had destroyed what weapons and arms they could discover they withdrew back to Boston, but were severely harassed by militiamen, who would later be known as 'Minutemen' because of the speed with which they could assemble. The first day's fighting had cost the British army seventy-three killed, 174 wounded and twenty-six missing. The colonists had lost ninety-three killed, wounded and missing. The first round had been won by the militia against regular, well-trained troops.

The War of Independence, sometimes called the American Revolution, had broken out between American colonists and Britain, and on 15 June, barely two months after the incident at Concord, the second Continental Congress recognised the colonial forces besieging Boston as a Continental Army. The siege would last until March 1776, by which time the besieging force had reached 20,000 men. The new Colonial Army was authorised to raise troops and the man appointed to command the army was Colonel (later General) George Washington. It was a fierce and bloody war, divided into campaigns with pitched battles and a high loss of life. The colonists had a ready reserve of volunteers to fill the ranks, not all of whom were willing or ready to fight, but they knew their duty and took up arms.

The British army on the other hand had to transport their replacement troops across the Atlantic by ship. One typical contingent sailed on 31 March 1776 with '… officers, sergeants, corporals, drummers, fifers and private men…' of the 21st Regiment of Foot (later to become the Royal Scots Fusiliers) embarking at Plymouth. This was one of many such voyages which sailed to America, as reinforcements were required for the war which would drag on until 1783. The journey took over 100 days to sail across the Atlantic. Storms led to deaths as men were washed overboard and other losses came through illness and disease, such as dysentery, due to the poor hygiene and diets on the vessel. The British army was experienced, well trained and well equipped, with recruits coming over to replace losses incurred in battle; losses such as the 1,000 casualties at the siege of Boston and the 590 killed and wounded at the Battle of Brandywine in September 1777. Earlier losses at engagements such as Bunker's Hill, where 410 British were killed or wounded compared to the American losses of some 800 in June 1775, had been small relative to other engagements, but even so all losses had to be made good.

Although a new and relatively inexperienced force, the Continental Army of George Washington had to be organised along the lines of an existing standing army of the day. The best examples to follow were either the British or French. The former were the enemy, but that is not to say that lessons could not be learnt from them. The French on the other hand were supporters of the colonists in their War of Independence and they also supplied weapons along with other equipment. Washington had to train his men as infantry, gunners had to be trained as artillerymen and even drummers had to be recruited and trained. One such boy to join Washington's forces was Rufus Landon from Litchfield County in Connecticut, who at the time of his enlistment in February 1776 was 17 years old. He was posted to Fort Ticonderoga in New York, serving as a drummer to Captain John Bigelow and a company of artillery. Although he became eligible for release from the ranks by November 1776, young Rufus remained in the army and served with another unit. He saw action in a number of skirmishes and actually survived the war, living until 1849, by which time he was around 90 years old.

Another 17-year-old boy to enlist as a drummer with the Continental Army was John George from Raritan in New Jersey. John joined Captain John Flahaven's company of Colonel Mattias Ogden's First New Jersey Battalion on 1 January 1777. By 8 November he is recorded in the company roll as being a drummer, by which time he had seen at least one minor skirmish at Clay Creek. At around this time each infantry regiment in the Continental Army had a drum-major, with at least one drummer per company, and they took to the battlefield with their respective companies and battalions when fighting. During the siege of Charleston during April and May 1777, the defending garrison of the Continental Army under Brigadier Benjamin Lincoln resisted the British attacks. However, he came to realise his position was hopeless and the British artillery was relentless. On 11 May he ordered a drummer onto the ramparts to beat out a signal to call for a parley to discuss terms of surrender. A Hessian Jaeger fighting for the British recalled how during '... this murdering and burning, I heard the sound of a drum'. Terms were agreed, the town surrendered and Brigadier Lincoln marched out with more than 5,600 troops, although he forced to abandon some 400 pieces of artillery. More than 130 years after Sherborne Castle had been surrendered following a drummer sounding a parley, the protocols of war were still being observed. In the British army there were volunteer units from the German states and returns from regiments such as the Hessen-Cassel and Hessan-Hanau in 1777–1778 show a total of eighty-three black drummers on the roster, some being as young as 12 or 13 years of age. This was a practice which had been established by earlier regiments, such as Evans's Dragoons in 1715, and, as we have seen, would continue with the famous black corps of drums in the 29th Regiment of Foot and well into the nineteenth century.

John George's military service then saw him being posted to the Maxwell Brigade, which was under the personal command of George Washington, and here he is still recorded as being a drummer and receiving a monthly wage of $7.30. Although his three-year enlistment period was up in 1780, John George elected to remain with his unit for the duration of the war. It is known that he was present at Yorktown in October 1781 when the British, under the command of General Cornwallis, surrendered. He would probably have seen Cornwallis march out, being granted the honour of marching at the head of the column with flags flying and drums beating. There was a certain irony in the tune being played by the British as they marched out, which according to most accounts was called 'The World Turned Upside Down'. Like his counterpart, Rufus Landon, John George lived to an old age and died in 1847. Both these incidents relate to young men serving as drummers, and the fact that John George attained the rank of sergeant indicates that although some drummers did indeed begin their careers at a young age, they could grow to become men and rise through the ranks. The American War of Independence finally ended in 1783 and the British army, along with the French, took the opportunity to withdraw.

Ten months before Cornwallis' surrender at Yorktown, the French had tried to carry the war closer to Europe by invading the 45 square mile island of Jersey in the British Channel Islands. The invasion of 1781 was not the first time the island had been invaded by France, despite having little military importance. Apart from serving as a naval base from where French ships could sail to harass British merchantmen sailing through the Channel, the islands had little or no strategic value. In the early hours of 6 January 1781, a French force under the command of Baron de Rullecourt landed on the eastern end of the island and quickly made its way to the town centre in the parish of St Helier. Facing this invasion were regular British troops from the Black Watch and the 42nd Regiment of Foot (later to become the Sherwood Foresters), along with other regiments including the local Jersey Militia. Events unfolded throughout the morning, with the French taking several prominent individuals prisoner in the hope that they could use them to negotiate the garrison on the island to surrender. For this purpose they also used drummers under flags of truce to convey parleys and call for the surrender of places such as Elizabeth Castle, which was well defended. However, Major Peirson rallied the local troops to face the French in a final confrontation in the place today known as the Royal Square. During the close-fought battle both Peirson and de Rullecourt were killed. It was a moment of triumph for the Jersey Militia in helping to win a battle on local soil. The drummers of this unit wore distinctive uniforms and the motif of a drum on their headdress. The funeral cortege for Major Peirson was accompanied by ten drummers and hundreds of troops he had commanded when his coffin was carried to the Parish Church in St Helier on 10 January 1781. It was a sad day for the island, but also a great relief that the threat from France had been removed. The Battle of Jersey may have been a side-show but the use of drummers as messengers showed they still had a value in the conduct of war on the small scale, as well as the grand scale.

In England it was recognised that it would only a question of time before war called on the army again and so the time was used to fill the ranks and prepare, with new weapons being issued. Within six years of withdrawing its support from its American ally, France found itself torn apart as revolution erupted in 1789 with the 'mob' turning on the nobility and imprisoning King Louis XVI

and other court officials. Within several years, new military commanders such as
Wellington and Napoleon Bonaparte would rise to replace those of the former
years such as Marlborough and Marshal Vendome. Britain and France would go
to war again as the eighteenth century ended and the nineteenth century began.
Armies would be on the move again across Europe and that meant the sound of
drummers would be heard as the soldiers marched and the campaigns unfolded.

THE RISE OF THE REGIMENTS

Armies for many centuries had been made up of various basic formations and specialist troops such as the Greek phalanx, a unit sixteen ranks wide and sixteen ranks deep, 224 men in all, and each equipped with an 18ft lance called a *sarisa*. These troops were the *pezhetairoi* (infantrymen) and along with other infantry units such as the hoplites and the cavalry, called the *cataphract*, were the standard Greek battle formations. The Roman army was formed of legions and *centuriae* and, later, the Norman army of Duke William of Normandy faced the shield wall of the *huscarl* of King Harold of England, who stood against the invasion at Senlac in Sussex near to modern-day Hastings and the name by which the decisive battle is more commonly known. On 16 October 1066 Duke William's forces fought a bitter and bloody battle, almost wiping out the English fyrd formed by the Anglo-Saxon militia in Harold's army.

The two main elements of any army at that time were the infantry and cavalry, and this remained the case until the Crusades were mounted by European armies united against the Muslim forces from 1096 onwards. During this protracted series of campaigns, many new and valuable lessons in warfare were learned, including the importance of specialist engineers and pioneers for assaulting besieged walled cities and castles. It was during the Crusades that European armies encountered the drum in battle for the first time. Eventually they were adopted by the Europeans for signalling and the spread of the drums was assured. It was not just the large states which adopted the drum, even small islands with a local militia force incorporated drums into the unit. For example, the tiny island of Sark in the Channel Islands, measuring barely 2 square miles, used drummers, who wore a uniform of scarlet-faced blue. Apart from the uniform, very little else is known about the drummers on Sark, except that in a letter dated 19 April 1794 we learn there were '… 2 drummers and 2 fifes whose clothing should be distinguished as is usual'. The Sark Militia was disbanded in 1875, but an old photograph shows Band Master Henri Le Feuvre in full uniform and baton, who would have been responsible for the drummers at the time.

Archers had been used for many centuries, including in the Greek, Persian and Roman armies in ancient times. However, it was not until the Middle Ages that archers began to rise in prominence, using the short bow, crossbow and later the longbow. These archers were known to the French as francs-archers, which were a force been created by King Charles VII between 1448 and 1451. Other mercenary groups came from Switzerland and the *Landsknechte* from the Germanic states who fought for Charles the Bold, Duke of Burgundy.

Before either of these last groups had been formed, there had been the Hussites, who took their name in memory and honour after their leader Jan Hus, executed in 1415. He was replaced as leader of the group by Jan Zizka (sometime written as Ziska), who continued to attack across modern-day Czech Republic in a series of 'Great Raids'. Using the tactic of forming their armoured wooden wagons into defences called *wagenburg*, they were armed with early hand guns and artillery to fight off any attackers. The Hussites included cavalry, infantry and artillery, each unit of which was trained to respond to signals relayed by drums and flags. On the march, the Hussites maintained their morale by singing religious songs with such gusto that the noise was known to unnerve their opponents; on one such occasion, historian Count Lutzow recorded that on seeing the Hussite forces and hearing them bellowing the song 'All ye warriors of God': 'No resistance was even attempted and before a single shot had been fired the whole German army, seized by a sudden panic, fled in the greatest disorder'. When Jan Zizka died in 1424, legend has it that he ordered his corpse to be excoriated and the skin used to cover the battle drums, so that even in death he might continue to lead the Hussites in battle. As patriotic as it sounds, it is unlikely that his macabre dying wish was ever completed in the sense that he may have wanted. Human skin can be treated and tanned to be turned into leather, but it is not as durable as calfskin and would not be capable of withstanding the pounding as a drumhead. Therefore, what may have happened is that if Zizka's skin was removed and preserved for leather as a drum skin, it was probably overlaid on top of a more traditional calfskin drumhead for added strength. This was not the only incidence of human skin being used for drumheads; it is recorded that the sixteenth-century Incan emperor, Huascar, felt so offended by the messenger sent by his brother Atahualpak, against whom he was fighting for dominance, that he ordered the man to be flayed and his skin used to cover drums. In a society renowned for its culture of human sacrifice, such incidents would have not been questioned. There would have certainly been sufficient skin taken from a man's back and chest to furnish enough leather for a drum.

By the sixteenth century, the first proper regiments were being formed in armies and terms such as 'colonel', derived from column or 'colonna', were being used in Italy. Change occurred rapidly and traditions were being established which would later become regimental customs. For example, following an engagement against French forces on the island of St Lucia, the 5th Regiment of Foot (later to become the Northumberland Fusiliers) were permitted to collect plumes from the headdress of the fallen French and place them in their own caps as a memento of the battle. The red and white plume has since become the symbol of the Royal Regiments of Fusiliers in the British army. Uniforms were beginning to be standardised to distinguish the armies in battle, and regimental flags or Colours were being used as rallying points for different units. The 5th Regiment of Foot was presented with a set of Colours known as the 'Drummer's Colours' following their part in the victory at the Battle of Wilhelmstahl during the Seven Years' War. Drums and fifes were attached to these new units for the purpose of marching in step and the drums were considered to be second in level of importance after the Regimental Colours, both of which should be protected from loss at all costs during battle. Over the next 200 years there would also be an evolution in weaponry and new forms of weapons were introduced, while older forms, such as the longbow, were declared obsolete. Gunpowder artillery brought about huge changes and special artillery regiments were raised. The bayonet would eventually replace the pike on the battlefield, although it would remain for a time as the sergeants' spontoon, which was a lance used to defend the Regimental Colours. The matchlock musket would also later be replaced by the more reliable flintlock musket. The drummers had to adapt to fit in with all of these changes and even evolve new tactics on the battlefield brought about by the advances in weaponry.

The new regiments served in a variety of roles and had names such as hussars, fusiliers (to protect the artillery), grenadiers, light infantry, dragoons (mounted infantry), Cossacks, chasseurs, carabineers, cuirassiers and many others, including elite bodyguards such as the Russian Imperial Guard raised by Peter the Great around 1720. Then there were the 'Blue Prussians', named after the colour of their tunics, but they were also known as the 'Giants of Potsdam'. The men who served in this regiment had to be at least 7ft in height if they were to be considered for the duty of personal bodyguard to Frederick William of Prussia. If no recruits of the required height could be found then he would purchase them, as he did a number of Irishman for whom he is understood to have paid the sum of £6,000 (approximately £360,000 by modern standards). In 1740, his son, Frederick II (better known as Frederick the Great) increased the size of this regiment to three battalions.

During the Russo-Prussian War, also known as the Seven Years' War, the armies of the two countries fought at the Battle of Zorndorf on 25 August 1758. Frederick the Great commanded a force of around 25,000 and was marching to the relief of Custria, which was being besieged by a Russian force of around 40,000 men commanded by Count Fermor. Frederick attacked and managed to defeat the Russians, who stubbornly stood their ground. The Russians had been alerted to the approach of the Prussian army by the sound of their marching music, yet despite this advance warning they were not able to make better preparations to fight the Prussians.

A Protestant pastor serving the needs of the Russian troops recorded how: 'The menacing beat of the Prussian drums was carried to our ears. For a time the woodwind was inaudible, but as the Prussians approached, we could hear the oboes playing the well-known hymn "*Ich bin ja, Herr, in deiner Macht!*" I cannot express what I felt at that instant but I do not think people will consider it off when I say that never since in the course of my long life have I heard that tune without experiencing the utmost emotion.'

Mounted regiments of infantry known as dragoons were raised for European armies, with France being one of the main proponents of this style of soldier. They would eventually become part of the cavalry, but initially not all commanders had faith in them as soldiers. In France the Duc de Rohan believed: '… they ruined the infantry, every man desiring to have a nag (horse) so that he might be fitter to rob and pillage'. In later years, South American armies, such as Argentina, raised regiments based on European lines, creating dragoon regiments which also had their own drummers. Dragoons are believed to have been first raised in France in the sixteenth century as mounted infantry. Their usefulness in battle would be questioned by some, but at the Battle of Hohenfriedberg in June 1745 during the War of Austrian Succession, when the Prussian Bayreuth Dragoons charged the Austro-Saxon army at a decisive point in the engagement, they proved successful and captured five pieces of artillery, sixty-seven Colours and took 2,500 prisoners. The British army followed this example and raised regiments of dragoons, but the reputation of these was never held in wide regard. Despite this the British army continued to use dragoon regiments and although trumpeters were being used by these regiments in 1766, we learn in a warrant dated two years later on 1 July 1768 that: 'The drums of the Dragoon Guards and Dragoons [are] to be of brass; the front, or forepart, to be painted with the colour of the facing of the regiment, upon which is to be the badge or rank of the regiment as in the second guidon. The banners of the kettledrum [are] … to be of the colour of the facing of the regiment, with the badge of the regiment, or its rank in the centre… as on the second standard'. The dragoons were following the example set by other regiments in decorating their drums with Regimental Colours, battalion or squadron number and battle honours, which had to be applied as part of regimental tradition. In much later times the reputation of the dragoons would be reconsidered and their true value recognised.

Saxony was another of those states which saw fit to raise regiments of dragoons and the regiments also included mounted drummers. These were not kettledrummers as in usual cavalry regiments, but rather used side drums. When preparing to mount in readiness for action the drummers were the last to mount and the first to dismount having been given a signal from their commanding officer. In Saxon dragoon regiments, a staff had a drummer attached to it and each of the six companies, formed with ninety-five men, had two drummers attached to them. The drum-major and the band of company drummers would march at the head of the band on ceremonial parades. The emergent Hussar regiments, raised from Hungarian influence, also had drummers, whose role it was to summon riders to assemble around regimental flags. Kettledrummers were usually part of the regimental bands and the instruments could be up to 3ft in diameter. The horses used for the kettledrums were often of a different colour from the rest of the regiment, such as the grey horses ridden by the French Mameluke-style units.

British regiments from around the eighteenth century, such as the Foot Guards, were beginning to wear distinctive 'mitre' caps, which were also being commonly worn among other European armies, and the drummers were wearing tunics of various colours trimmed with lace. The uniforms of the British and French armies would become familiar sights on other continents, such as America and India, where the two countries would fight for territorial gains. Drummers were by now beating out a single tap on the drum to match a man's pace on the march and the tempo was set for different speeds at which a regiment was required to march. Ordinary time was set at seventy-five paces per minute and quick time was set at around 108 paces per minute. A third speed of marching was 'double time', set at 120 paces per minute, and that was used by the new light infantry regiments being raised, such as the Highland Light Infantry from Scotland. Drummers could not beat out at that speed and so buglers played for the regiment to march by, a custom still kept today by some regiments such as the Gurkha Rifles in the British army.

The drums themselves at this time were being made using either wood or metal to form the shells or bodies, over which the skin or drumhead was stretched. The wooden drum shells were made from vertical lengths of wood such as beech, ash or maple, shaped and cut to size, and formed into a barrel-like shape through cooperage techniques, like those used in the storage of wine or dry goods such as gunpowder. Examples of these types of drums can be found in museums across Europe and America, and are highly decorated. For example, at Le Musée de l'Empéri in France one particular drum is known to have been made in 1756 from marks on the interior of the drum shell, which also bears the stamp 'faiseur de caisses', meaning 'maker of boxes (cases)', and places it in the reign of King Louis XV. It is painted in the colours of the Royal Roussillon Infantry Regiment and fitted with rope tensions to adjust the drum skin. Metal drum shells were made from either copper or brass sheet which has been rolled into a tube and the ends fitted together. Brass is an alloy made from a process using copper and zinc and is known to have been developed around several thousand years BC, making it one of the earliest metals to be worked by artisans to produce a range of artefacts such as pots, ornaments, helmets, weapons and armour. The knowledge to work these metals also led to drum shells being produced and brass continued to be used for this purpose for thousands of years. Pottery drum shells have been discovered at archaeological sites around the world, including Moravia where the remnants of such drums have been dated to around 6,000BC. These drums, however, would have been for purely ceremonial purposes, and military drums would have been made from either wood or metal for added durability.

THE NAPOLEONIC PERIOD

In France after the Revolutionary Wars, the army would eventually be commanded by Napoleon Bonaparte and become more efficient and ever-more colourful to match that of other European armies. This was going to be an age of splendour, but also of great hardships and seemingly endless warfare: in the twenty-one years of fighting from 1793 to 1814, France would lose an estimated 1.7 million soldiers either killed on the battlefields or as victims of disease. Napoleon formed many new regiments, including elite units such as the 'Old Guard', which would virtually become an army itself. The Grenadier Guards of the French '*La Vieille Garde Imperiale*' had to be at least 5ft 10in tall and were required to serve for a period of ten years. They wore large bearskin caps which measured 12in in height and gave the wearers greater prominence in stature. The uniform comprised a blue tunic with red cuffs and white lapels, red epaulets and copper buttons. The regiment had a 'battery' of twenty-four drums and the regimental band had forty-six musicians. The drum-major wore a similar uniform, except that his buttons were gilt, he wore a large scarlet sash embroidered in gilt and in his bearskin cap included a large tricoloured plume. Drummers with kettledrums were also attached to the Horse Grenadiers and, being a mounted regiment, trumpeters were used in place of the corps of drums and were attired in blue tunics with crimson lapels, cuffs and ribbons with stripes of gold. They wore a bicorn hat in place of the bearskin cap. The kettledrummer rode at the head of this formation wearing a similar uniform but dressed like a hussar, with a blue dolman draped over a shoulder and his trousers were crimson. The regiment of Horse Grenadiers would fight in every campaign from Marengo on 14 June 1800 to Waterloo on 18 June 1815. Napoleon famously once said to the Austrian diplomat Prince Metternich: 'You can't stop me... I spend 30,000 men a month'. He was, of course, referring to the losses incurred in fighting his campaigns across Europe, from the coast of Spain and Portugal in the west to Moscow in the east and Egypt in the south. It has been calculated that between 1804 and 1813 Napoleon conscripted over 2.4 million troops, all of whom had to be issued with a uniform and properly equipped, including drummers.

Napoleon Bonaparte had been a prominent figure before taking command of the army and France in 1799. Ten years earlier in 1789, when the French Revolution erupted with the 'storming of the Bastille', Napoleon Bonaparte was a young, newly commissioned junior officer in the Royalist army. He had attended the *Ecole Militaire* (Military School) in 1784 and joined a regiment of artillery in 1785. Eight years later, in September 1793, during the period of France's Revolutionary Wars, Napoleon was by now a captain and was sent to the city of Toulon with orders to drive out the British garrison. It was not entirely by chance that he was given the task, as he had used his political connections to obtain the posting and his Republican sentiments, despite having obtained a commission in the royal army of King Louis XVI, must have also helped. He was promoted to brigadier-general and had forced the British out of Toulon by late December. However, it was not to last and he was dismissed after falling from favour. He did not have to wait long for his next opportunity, which came in October 1795 when an uprising threatened the *Directoire executive*, or Directory, the governing body of France after the Revolution. Directory member Paul Barras sent for General Bonaparte to protect the Convention from the hostile crowds. He had 5,000 men under his command and dispersed the crowds by turning the guns of the artillery on them and giving them a 'whiff of grapeshot'. He was rewarded for his efforts by being put in command of the army of Italy, a less than crack unit which was on the verge of mutiny, being short of supplies such as clothing and going unpaid during its operations in the Ligurian Alps; it was little wonder that they were reluctant soldiers.

He wasted no time and, using his youthful energy and personality, he set about transforming the army into a semblance of a fighting unit. Napoleon has had the term genius applied to him on numerous occasions over the past 200 years and, indeed, he often displayed the ability to turn around seemingly hopeless situations with his strategies and grasp of tactics. He could speak to his troops in such a manner that he could inspire them to continue to fight. The Duke of Wellington believed that Napoleon's presence on the battlefield was worth 40,000 troops. They only ever faced one another across the battlefield once, but commanders of such calibre could appreciate each other's capabilities. One of Napoleon's first moves on taking over the army in Italy was to promise his troops that they would be paid, before seeing to it that they were fed and equipped with boots, uniforms and weapons. With morale raised he set out on his campaign in April 1796, moving against the Austrians and fighting a series of engagements across Italy which within a year would see Vienna suing for peace. It was during this campaign that he formulated his tactic known as the '*manoeuvre sur les derrieres*' (manoeuvre on the behind), meaning the envelopment of the enemy forces by moving to encircle them. He employed it many times during the fifty or so major battles during his career. Another tactic he formulated was the '*masse de rupture*' (breaking of the mass) and this involved a breakthrough of the enemy's rank by force of numbers. Future commanders would use these tactics, and those of Frederick the Great, to produce their own version in the twentieth century using motorised vehicles and artillery in great numbers.

The early battles in which Napoleon Bonaparte saw action was a period known as the Wars of the Revolution, and to fill the ranks of the army and provide the equipment and support necessary for the continuation of the war, the whole of France was conscripted '*levée en masse*' (massed uprising). By early 1794, some 750,000 troops were under arms and civilians were engaged in providing services for the troops, such as producing uniforms, boots and weapons. Other European countries began to recruit troops to the ranks, including England where soldiers joined the army of their own free will, although the Royal Navy used a method called the 'press gang' to virtually kidnap recruits. The British army never resorted to such tactics nor did it implement conscription, instead remaining committed to enlisting volunteer recruits. Due to France's military preparedness and planned expansion, the reputation of the army as a fighting force, combined with the weight of the whole country behind it, made it the most dominant force in Europe. The first campaign undertaken by France was in Italy and was conducted between 1796 and 1797, where General Napoleon Bonaparte showed his true prowess. He was energetic and fearless, two characteristics which he would come to display at the Battle of Arcola from 15 to 17 November 1796.

Having reinvigorated the French army in Italy and reorganised and re-equipped it, Napoleon had been on campaign and marched many hundreds of miles across Italy by the time he reached the Austrian positions at Arcola. Napoleon had some 20,000 men to face the Austrian army of around 24,000 men under the command of Baron Josef Alvintzy. All attempts to storm the bridge had been repulsed and on 17 November, the third day of the battle, the attack was renewed. The legend of André Estienne swimming the river to beat his drum so loudly that the Austrians believed they were surrounded has an element of truth in it, but there was much more to the story than is told to tourists visiting the town of Cadenet. That day, General Pierre Augereau managed to cross the river Alpone further downstream from the bridge at Arcola. Using a trestle bridge he managed to get his troops over while another diversionary assault was being led by André Masséna. A French cavalry detachment also managed to work its way round to the rear of the Austrian positions and with bugles blowing, and no doubt young André Estienne beating his drum, the Austrians gave way and deserted their positions. The battle had cost the French 5,000 captured, killed and wounded, but the Austrians had lost more than 6,000 men killed, captured and wounded. The Austrian General Paul Davidovich found himself being pursued by Napoleon, who maintained the pressure and forced the Austrians back. Not letting up the pressure, the French continued and by March 1797 they were in Austria itself. By October the Treaty of Campo Formio brought to an end to the war between France and Austria, and after this much-needed French victory Napoleon's reputation in the army was cemented.

Returning from his successful campaign in Italy, Napoleon spent a brief interlude as the commanding officer of the army on the French coast which was massing for the invasion. The French *Directoire* expected him to remain at this post, but Napoleon had other ideas and put forward his own plans, outlining a campaign to invade Egypt from where French forces could attack England's trade routes with India and extend its influence across the Mediterranean Sea. In July 1798 the French invasion fleet set sail for Egypt with Napoleon in command. Whilst en route, a squadron of warships were diverted from the fleet to attack and capture the island of Malta.

The campaign in Egypt brought Europeans and Mamelukes face to face once again. This was the very region from where the influence of drums had originally spread out to enter the culture of European military regimes and manifest so prominently in the highly militarised state of France, where drums and drummers would reach unprecedented levels on the battlefield. The Egyptian campaign began well for the French, who consolidated their positions and captured the capital city of Cairo. However, Horatio Nelson led a fleet of Royal Navy warships to destroy the French fleet on 1 August 1798, severing the lines of supply to the army. This threw the French plans into disarray, but Napoleon remained in Egypt and continued to campaign tenaciously, scoring a number of successes in battle in 1799, which not only further enhanced his military reputation, but also elevated the fighting capability of the French army in adverse conditions. The Duke of Wellington, who would only ever face Napoleon across the battlefield once in his military career, would later say of the French commander: 'I suspect all the continental armies are half beaten before the battle begins', which must surely have been the case when witnessing the impressive ranks of musketeers, blocks of cavalry and batteries of artillery. Napoleon finally returned to France in August 1799, but the French forces would remain in Egypt for a further two years until the British army, with Turkish support, forced the remainder of the French out of the country. As for the Mamelukes themselves, their end finally came when the Turkish Governor, Mohammed Ali, ordered that all the *beys*, the senior commanders, be murdered. Without their leadership the force grew weaker and finally dissolved.

Over the next fifteen years Napoleon's armies would march the length and breadth of the European mainland, and his brand of military expertise would be exported to influence the military doctrine of many countries, including America. Under his leadership, French troops would take on all comers in battle, including Prussian, Austrian, Spanish and Italian forces. The British army under Arthur Wellesley, the Duke of Wellington, was able to tie down French troops in Spain and Portugal, where the Peninsular War on the Iberian peninsular was fiercely contested. Napoleon reorganised the French army and incorporated allied forces, which joined him in his conquests. At around this time, a typical demi-brigade of the French army or regiment of three battalions included one drum-major, one drum corporal and eight musicians at staff level. Each of

1 – Drummers depicting the use of drums in the fifteenth century. There is ample evidence that drums were used on the battlefield at this time.

2 – Drummers on the battlefield in the medieval period were still a relatively innovative move in military evolution.

3 – The statute of André Estienne in his home town of Cadenet in memory of his actions at the Battle of Arcola.

4 – Standard bearers were used to pass signals and also served as a rallying point in the medieval period.

5 – Drums were used as a means of signalling during the eighteenth century as depicted by these re-enactors.

6 – During the Napoleonic Wars drummers in all armies relayed signals and kept morale during long marches.

7 – These drummers of the recreated 78th Highland Regiment from Canada depict the use of drums during the Victorian period.

8 – Before the introduction of the field telephone semaphore flags were still used as well as drums for signalling purposes.

9 – A recreated drummer from the eighteenth century. He is wearing the small bearskin cap of the style worn during the period.

10 – Recreated drummers depict the use of the drum during the period of the Victorian army.

11 – Drummers were used extensively during the American Civil War as depicted by these re-enactors.

12 – Modern French army drummers show the ceremonial duties performed after many centuries of being associated with the military.

13 – The Corps of Drums leads the band of the modern French army showing the ceremonial duties of the drums today.

14 – Street entertainers from South America with drums showing how drums have a use at all levels today as civilian entertainers, as well as with the military.

15 – British attack on Cuidad Rodrigo on 19 January 1812 where General Robert Craufurd was killed. He was a strict disciplinarian and advocated flogging.

16 – German army drummers on parade on the outbreak of the First World War in August 1914.

17 – Ceremony to return the drum to the Gordon Highlanders which had been left behind during the retreat to Dunkirk in 1940.

18 – Corps of Drums of the 2nd Battalion Norfolk Regiment marching through Alton in Hampshire *c.*1895.

19 – Drum-Major William Kenny of the Gordon Highlanders, who won the Victoria Cross for rescuing wounded men during the fighting around Ypres in October 1914.

20 – The Chivers Drums and the drums recovered after the retreat to Dunkirk on display at the Wiltshire Regimental Museum in Salisbury, Wiltshire.

21 – Drummer of the recreated
57th Regiment of Foot (Middlesex
Regiment) carrying his drum on his
back using drag ropes.

22 – Drummers and Colours of the 3rd
Battalion Lancashire Fusiliers *c.*1900.

23 – Flamboyant uniform of the black drummers of the 29th Regiment of Foot.

24 – French *Zouaves* drummers on the march in the way they would have looked during the Crimean War.

25 – Drummer of the Northumberland Fusiliers around the time of the First World War. He wears his drummers proficiency badge on his left sleeve.

26 – Scene depicting an incident during the Siege of Tarragona in Spain on 3–11 June 1813. The artist shows the drums at an improbable angle which would not have allowed them to be played properly.

27 – The remains of Sherborne Castle where the Parliamentarian drummer conducting the parlay in 1645 was almost hanged for his impudence.

28 – State visit to France by Tsar Nicholas II of Russia in September 1901. The French army has paraded a band with drummers for the ceremonial duties.

29 – Three young Guards drummer boys in winter greatcoats c.1870.

30 – Regimental drums and colours of the Royal Jersey Light Infantry at the regimental museum at Elizabeth Castle on Jersey.

The Battle of Jersey. Fought 1781.

54105.

31 – The death of Major Peirson during the Battle of Jersey in January 1781. His funeral cortege included many drummers.

32 – Recreated German army drummer from the First World War. He wears the distinctive shoulder devices known as 'Swallows' Nests' and would have tapped out the beat during route marches.

these battalions had a strength of around 1,000 men and were for
unit known as an '*ordre mixte*', which included eighteen drummers
This was the French corps of drums for three battalions and the reg
be made up from different units such as fusiliers, *voltigeur* (elite skirmishers) an
grenadiers, with a *tambour maitre* (drum master or drum-major). At one point in
the 1790s, the French army had plans for 196 such demi-brigades, on paper at
least, and working on the structural organisation of these units there would have
been 196 drum-majors, 196 drum corporals and 10,584 drummers. It would be
the beat of such drummers that the French troops would hear on the march from
Spain to Prussia and even further afield.

The fifes and drums of the corps of drums remained separate from the regimental band, which could be made up of some twenty musicians, including a bass
drum (sometimes referred to as a 'base drum'). The term 'drummer boy' was still
being used as a general term, even though some drummers could be veterans of
several campaigns and therefore adult men. French troops often sang whilst on
the march and Prussian, Austrian and even Russian troops also sang as a means to
keep up morale on marches. The drummers carried side drums suspended from
their left hips, but when not required to play and when the march was particularly gruelling, a drummer could carry his drum strapped to his back over his
knapsack using special attachment straps.

Bugles were beginning to gain more significance as a means of passing signals
on the battlefield. The distinctive sound it produced could be carried over a distance of around 3 miles and still be distinguished. This was necessary because the
battlefield was becoming increasingly noisier as artillery was being deployed in
ever-greater numbers and muskets were fired in volleys which could drown out the
sound of a drum beat. Nevertheless, the drum continued to be used alongside the
bugle to relay a range of calls or signals for troops, such as the order to 'Advance',
'Halt', 'Cease Fire' and 'Retreat'. Other signals included 'Fire', 'Extend', Close', 'Lie
Down' (to avoid artillery fire), 'Call in Skirmishers' and of course 'Drill', 'Fatigues'
and 'Officers' Dinner'. The British army during these wars against France was sub-
sidising many of its allies either with money or weapons and equipment. Between
1813 and 1814, one return for equipment included some 624 drums and bugles,
along with standards and other regimental accoutrements.

In 1811 Napoleon's sphere of influence extended from Spain in the west, north-
wards to Denmark, Sweden and Norway, and eastwards to the Austrian Empire
and the borders of Russia. Having learnt lessons from the expedition in Egypt
and the prospect of the British army just a few miles across the English Channel,
itself dominated by the Royal Navy which also blockaded French trade routes,
Napoleon decided to concentrate all his efforts on campaigns on the European
mainland. In 1812 he began to lay plans for his most ambitious campaign to date
and between May and June that year he assembled an army of some 450,000 men
in the Grand Duchy of Warsaw, present-day Poland, in readiness to invade Russia.

The attack against Russia began on 24 June and Napoleon's axis of advance had the Russian capital city of Moscow very firmly in its sights; however, this prize lay more than 600 miles away. It was a hard-fought campaign with numerous fierce engagements, such as the Battle of Borodino on 7 September 1812 where the French lost some 28,000 men, but inflicted losses of around 52,000 killed, captured and wounded on the Russians. Just one week later, on 14 September, Napoleon entered Moscow with an almost exhausted army. Forced marches and hard fighting had given him his goal, but the cost had been great; he was many miles away from France at the end of a very fragile supply line, with few if any reliable means of receiving logistical support or reinforcements.

The occupation of Moscow was a short-lived victory and fires broke out in parts of the city which soon spread out of control, resulting in the destruction of buildings which could otherwise have served as billets for his troops. Winter was setting in and, with food and fuel for his men and horses in short supply, Napoleon realised he had to withdraw. The retreat from Moscow has become a byword for extreme suffering and not without good cause. The long march back to France began in early November for the 100,000 men with Napoleon. Starving, freezing and harassed at every turn, the retreating French army was in tatters and losing more men every day. On 8 December Napoleon left the main column and struck out for France, leaving his army to fend for itself. Eventually only some 10,000 of the original force which marched out of Moscow would make it back to France. One of those who perished on the retreat from Moscow was Drum-Major Siliakus, a Dutchman who served with the 3rd Regiment. Standing at over 6ft 6in tall, he cut a dashing figure and was very prominent. It has been opined that some French drum-majors, because of their appearance, were just as famous as some of Napoleon's better-known generals and probably even more so than some of the lesser officers. For example, other outstanding drum-majors included Vercellana, who stood over 6ft in height and served with Napoleon's elite unit, the Old Guard. There was also Benjamin Denelle and Senot, who both served with the Imperial Guard in 1804 in the the 1st Foot Grenadier Regiment, and of whom Napoleon said: 'My beautiful and honest Senot'. This dashing man had been painted by leading artists of the time, such as Raffet, and his name was well-known across France. Senot survived the campaigns and died in 1837. Despite Napoleon's Russian tragedy, he was far from being a spent force and still constituted a threat to the peace of Europe; but with his enemies closing in, such as Austria, Britain, Prussia and Russia, it was only a question of time.

Meanwhile, on the other side of the Atlantic and at around the same time that Napoleon Bonaparte was invading Russia in June 1812, war broke out between Britain and America. While the British army conducted land battles in the European style with massed ranks, the war was pursued more vigorously at sea. Even so, the fighting extended up to the Canadian border and the war finally ended in January 1815. The Battle of New Orleans fought on 8 January 1815 was one of the last land engagements, but naval actions continued at sea until late March 1815. Present at the battle was a black drummer by the name of Jordan Noble. He is understood to have been born in Georgia in 1800, and as a free black man chose to enlist in the 7th Regiment of the US army in 1812, aged around 12. Noble served during the Louisiana campaign and had been present at several actions where his drumming relayed signals. He remained in the army after the war was over, transferring to the 1st Regiment Louisiana Volunteers and is recorded as serving during the time of the Mexican War of 1846–1848. When the American Civil War broke out in 1861, Jordan Noble helped recruit free blacks to serve in Confederate Militia units, by which time he was around 61 years of age. Noble again survived the conflict and is believed to have died in the mid-1880s with an incredible military record of service behind him. During the same war, the story goes that a young boy called Timothy Batchelder from Allenstown in New Hampshire, aged around 8 years old in 1812, accompanied the soldiers going off to fight the British. His story is well documented and his skill in playing the drum to inspire the troops is also well recorded. He marched with the troops to keep up morale and in later life he became a drum-major. Batchelder's and Noble's stories were but two which had similar antecedents and would be repeated many times again in the future. Timothy's grandfather, David Batchelder, had served in the military having marched 40 miles to join the British forces landing at Portsmouth in New Hampshire, and fought as a loyalist during the War of Independence. Another Batchelder, Henry, had served as a drummer during the same war and is known to have served in the 3rd Company, 2nd Regiment of Foot commanded by Colonel Enoch Poor from 1775. The war in America had been a protracted affair and diverted troops away from the main conflict in Europe, where Napoleon Bonaparte's career was coming to an end.

Throughout 1813, Napoleon undertook what has become known as the Leipzig Campaign and fought several engagements, including the Battle of Lutzen in May and the Battle of Dresden in August. During September and October the French lost actions against the Allies, who kept up the pressure and finally, at the Battle of Leipzig (sometimes called the Battle of the Nations) from 16 to 19 October, pushed the French back. Despite fighting a brilliant series of delaying actions in early 1814, the Allies were now on French soil and 11 April Napoleon unconditionally abdicated. His fate was to be exiled to the island of Elba and, although cut off, he busied himself with affairs and kept up to date with developments in France, especially the mood of the people and in particular the military.

Finally, in early 1815, he made his move and sailed from Elba, landing back in France on 1 March and arriving in Paris on 20 March after a march which drew many old soldiers back to the ranks. The next few weeks have become called 'The Hundred Days' and would see some of the finest military strategies to be conducted during the period. Napoleon set out from Paris on 11 June to begin his campaign and headed for Belgium. Actions at Quatre-Bras and Ligny on 16 June were to be overshadowed by the main engagement at Waterloo on 18 June, bringing Napoleon and the Duke of Wellington face to face across the battlefield for the first and only time.

The history of the Battle of Waterloo has been covered many times and there are some excellent works on the subject. In essence the Battle of Waterloo was conducted in several phases, which helps greatly in understanding the sprawling fighting which extended across the width of the Duke of Wellington's frontage of almost 5 miles. The Duke of Wellington had over 67,600 men in his army to face Napoleon's army of around 74,000 men. Each regiment of infantry on both sides had drummers as part of their organisation and from the thousands of fighting men engaged on the day of the battle, it can be calculated that there must have been hundreds of drummers among the ranks. Wellington had made his preparations and dispersed his troops, which included deploying units to defend the buildings at La Haye and Papelotte on his left, the walled farm at La-Haye-Sainte to his centre left and Hougoumont on his right. These defences were to protect Wellington's flanks against being turned and his centre from being penetrated, blunting Napoleon's tried and tested tactics. The battle commenced around 11.30am, although times vary from one account to another, but it is agreed the French opened the attack with an assault against Hougoumont, held by infantry including the Coldstream Guards. The location was a walled farm and throughout the day the French kept up a relentless attack against the position, eventually forcing the north gates open and allowing some thirty troops to enter the courtyard. The defenders managed to force the gates closed and one by one the French soldiers were cut down by the musket fire of the Guardsmen.

One of those who forced himself into Hougoumont was French Sous-Lieutenant Legros, nicknamed 'L'enfonceur' (The Smasher). By all accounts he was a giant man and, as a pioneer, carried an axe for the purpose of hacking away barricades, which was typical of pioneer troops even in the British army. When the gates were closed the ingress of further troops was halted and those already inside were left with nowhere to go and completely at the mercy of the British infantry. As they were killed one by one in this close-quarter action, cut off from the rest of the battle raging outside, including the magnificent Legros, only a small, nameless drummer boy was left as the sole survivor of the attack. Some accounts say the young boy had lost his drum, but one thing is certain and that is he was left unharmed by the soldiers defending Hougoumont. From his small stature and non-combatant status, the grown men knew that the young boy represented no threat and was probably terrified by the sight of men were being killed all round him.

The battle continued unabated until the early evening and the carnage was terrible. The Prussians riding to Wellington's support alerted the French to their approach by the sound of drums and bugles. This was during the last, closing stages of the battle and the Prussian General von Gneisenau pursued the retreating French with vigour to prevent any regrouping. He ordered a drummer to mount a captured French horse, ride after the withdrawing French troops and to beat his drum when he came across the enemy. It was finally all over with the French losses amounting to 25,000 killed and wounded. The Duke of Wellington had lost 15,000 killed and wounded, which later led to him writing: 'Nothing except a battle lost can be half so melancholy as a battle won'.

On 22 June 1815 Napoleon abdicated for the second and final time, being exiled to the remote island of St Helena in the South Atlantic, where he died on 5 May 1821, aged 51. As to the fate of the unknown drummer boy at Hougoumont, nothing appears to be heard of him. We therefore have to assume that after the battle he joined the thousands of other troops making their way back to their homes or depots. Europe after Napoleon could now begin to recover economically, with a degree of military stability returning and, apart from minor engagements such as the 'Oporto Revolution' in Portugal (1820) and the Russo-Turkish War (1828–1829), the period of peace in Europe would last until 1848. This trouble would spread to a number of European states such as France, Scandinavia and across the Atlantic to Brazil. The British army was able to distance itself from such strife and instead busied itself with overseas interests in Africa, India and the Middle East, where troops helped in maintaining the British Empire. France had entered into North Africa by invading Algiers in 1830, but all this was outside of European affairs. By the time of the next major crisis which involved European states, the Crimean War (1853–1856), further advances in technology once again changed the face of warfare and would affect the role of drummers both directly and indirectly.

AFTER NAPOLEON

rance had managed to hold on to overseas territories after the defeat of Napoleon Bonaparte and by the 1840s had even added to its empire with gains in North Africa, such as Algeria, where colourfully uniformed regiments of locally raised troops such as Turcos and Spahis were eventually integrated into the French army. These native regiments had drummers and trumpeters who would go on to serve in campaigns such as the Crimean War and continue well into the first half of the twentieth century. By now, virtually every army across Europe had its own Guards regiments, especially Grenadier, with the Italian units holding elite status. Even after the reform of King Victor Emmanuel I after 1821, the Grenadier Guards stood apart, especially the drummers whose original red tunics were now replaced by blue. *Shako* caps replaced the bearskin caps, but despite the change the regiment retained its fine status. In 1848, the 'Year of Revolution' as the Austrian diplomat Prince Metternich called it, several European states, including France and Italy, erupted in turmoil. In that year, Italian troops fought against Austrian troops along the Mincio River and in particular at Governolo where Italian trumpeters and drummers played so loudly the Austrians believing they were greatly outnumbered and immediately withdrew in a hurry. It would seem that the Austrians would never be able to forget the actions of young André Estienne and his fellow drummers only fifty years earlier.

By the second half of the nineteenth century, warfare had become industrialised on a scale never before imagined. Muzzle-loading muskets such as the Brown Bess and Charleville, used by the British and French respectively in so many previous campaigns, had by now been replaced by breech-loading rifles. The early paper cartridges had been replaced by brass cartridges and output from the armaments manufacturers had increased to produce prodigious levels of war materiel. By the 1850s, for example, the output of ammunition from the Woolwich Arsenal in London often exceeded 250,000 rounds or bullets per day. The designs of a new weapon referred to as 'machine-guns' also began to appear during this period. At first the rate of fire from these weapons was low, but later they would increase to fire hundreds of rounds per minute and, together with the new rifles, could use up the ammunition being produced. At the Battle of Waterloo in 1815, a good infantryman could fire his musket some three times per minute. These new rifles entering service, such as the British army's Snider-Enfield, increased an infantryman's firepower four-fold. Similar advances were being made in other armies and even in America new weapons were changing the methods of war. These new weapons combined with ever-more powerful artillery shells filled with high explosive compounds and detonated with such thunderous roars that they made the battlefield too noisy for the drum beat to be heard. What chance did the beat of a drum have against the cacophony of so many shells being fired at the same time as rifle and machine-gun fire was being unleashed? Bugles were being looked at as an option in many countries, such as England and France, and the instrument did eventually come to replace the drum, although not entirely.

However, the main development to bring about the greatest effect on the role of the drummer on the battlefield, which had been unquestioned for centuries, was the utilisation of the railways. If artillery and more powerful weaponry had made the battlefield a far noisier place for the drummer to be heard, then the introduction of this large, noisy engine would only add to the problem. The idea of using trains to move troops en masse and over vast distances in a fraction of the time it took an army to march was slow to catch on a first, but once proven, its adaptation by other nations was swift. The writings of military theorists such as the Swiss Antoine-Henri Jomini and the Prussian Carl von Clausewitz, whose respective works included the '*Precis de l'art de la Guerre*' (Precis on the Art of War) and '*Vom Kriege*' (On War), also helped to evolve military strategy in response to the changes in technology. These innovations would all come together and affect armies around the world, even as far as South America where the military tended to copy the trends set by their European counterparts.

A conflict of interest between Russia and Turkey led to the latter declaring war on 4 October 1853. This was not the first time the two countries had been at war, as only twenty-five years earlier the two nations had fought a war between 1828 and 1829, but since that time much had happened in each country. Russia's military power had increased whilst Turkey's had deteriorated, leading Tsar Nicholas I to refer to the country as 'The sick man of Europe'. However, he did not count on Turkey attracting such powerful allies as France and Britain, both of which declared war on Russia in March 1854. Over the next two-and-a-half years these two nations would bear the brunt of the war until February 1856 when the conflict ended.

The fighting would be confined to the Crimean Peninsular, a fierce and inhospitable terrain, and during the war new tactics and strategies were introduced, including trench warfare. In previous wars there had always been tactical movement and frontal assaults on strategic positions in the old ways of Napoleon Bonaparte, but here, in what was to become called the Crimean War, advances in weaponry would designate a new era of battlefield tactics. Drummers would accompany the attacking troops, but it was becoming evident that they were no longer as vital as in earlier wars. Artillery barrages fired continuously and cavalry charges, such as the British 'Heavy Brigade' and the ill-fated 'Light Brigade', were reported in national newspapers such as *The Times* of London for the public back home to read. During the Crimean War the circulation of *The Times* increased to 40,000 per day. Only forty years earlier, during the Napoleonic Wars, the newspaper had sold 5,000 copies per day, showing how important news had become to the civilian population.

The innovations developed during the Crimean War showed that warfare was changing at an unprecedented rate, and the end for the role of the drummer on the battlefield was also approaching. The Crimean War was the first conflict to be photographed, and telegraphy meant that it was the first war to have the news from the battlefield transmitted across thousands of miles to keep the public informed by dispatches from journalists such as William Russell of *The Times*. The Crimean War was also the first major conflict to involve European nations for almost half a century, but when it ended it opened the way for numerous wars to begin, and these too would be witnessed by civilians who photographed the events and by journalists, who sent written accounts of a battle in a number of hours rather than weeks.

The Crimean War was also to prove a turning point in other ways. The weapons may have changed to become more powerful and deployed in greater numbers, but the uniforms were from a bygone era and virtually unchanged from almost fifty years earlier. The French regiments, for example, which fought in the conflict included *Zouaves* from North Africa wearing brilliant red pantaloons, and many of the officers wore tunics bedecked in epaulets trimmed in gold. The British army sent the three Guards regiments: Grenadier, Coldstream and Scots, wearing scarlet tunics and bearskin caps, the only time they would fight a campaign wearing such uniform. Drummers were still dressed flamboyantly and their tunics trimmed with elaborate braid. The British and French were now allied against the Russians, who had once been the allies of Britain and the enemy of France. All this change was confusing for some of the older officers who still thought of the French as the 'enemy' and sometimes referred to them as such. These were the officers who had not seen a shot fired in anger for over forty years since the Battle of Waterloo and for them to know that Napoleon III, the nephew of Bonaparte, was Emperor of France could not have helped in their comprehension of the situation. Newspapers of the time reported that the troops embarking were the finest to have ever left British shores. William Russell of *The Times* reported that: 'Red is the colour, after all, and the white slashings of the breast of the coat and the cross belts, though rendering a man conspicuous enough, give him an appearance in size which other uniforms don't create'. It all sounded so noble, but on the battlefield these uniforms told the Russian troops in their dull grey uniforms where the Allies were assembling. In the winter months, grey became the universal colour as great coats were issued and blankets added for layers to give extra warmth.

Several months after the British army had sailed for the Crimea following the Battle of the Alma on 20 September 1854, William Russell would write of the achievements of the 93rd Highlanders that they were the '… thin red streak tipped with a line of steel…' He was referring to the regiment's steadfastness in facing up to Russian cavalry charges without resorting to the tactic of forming into squares, which was the traditional mode for infantry to repel cavalry. Over the years Russell's remarks have been corrupted into the phrase: 'the thin red line'. The original remarks gave artists back in England the inspiration to paint the scene showing heroic Scottish Highland troops fighting against such adversity. Indeed, Sir Colin Campbell, commanding the Highland Brigade at the Battle of Alma, including the 93rd Highlanders, spoke reassuringly to his troops saying: 'Now men, you are going into action. Remember this; whoever is wounded must lie where he falls until the bandsmen come to attend him'. This was a reminder that bandsmen and drummers were serving in the role as stretcher bearers, tasked with recovering the wounded from the battlefield and delivering them to the surgeons for treatment.

Even before the fighting began in earnest and as the Russians were assembling in their positions, reports were made how their singing and beating drums could be heard coming from their lines. The corps of drums accompanying the French and British troops were engaged in their traditional role of marching into battle. When the French attacked a position known as Mamelon, the initial assault was stopped, but it was restarted when reinforcements came up to support the assault. A junior British officer, Lieutenant William Young, wrote home how the French attacked resumed with: '… drums and bugles playing a rub-a-dub-dub you could hear a mile off, and they actually walked through the Mamelon. Not content with that, they must needs go on to attack the Malakoff or Round Tower, and then after a desperate fight they were driven back. However, they are now in the Mamelon'. The Malakoff would be attacked repeatedly and one French soldier serving with the 1st *Zouaves* recalled that an attack was launched to the: '… immense cry of "*Vive L'Empereur*"…' As this particular attack continued against the Malakoff, the French '… bugles and drums struck up their own racket…' It was inspiring but cost the French dearly as the numbers of killed and wounded mounted; an example that the days of such headlong rushes against modern weapons were numbered. One French assault nearly caught the Russians unprepared and the order to sound the alarm was given. However the Russian '… drummer had been killed and the alarm was sounded by the bugler standing by'. The drummer was now being replaced by the bugler, not just temporarily when he was killed or wounded, but because the sound was different and carried further amidst the noise of gunfire.

The Turkish troops used drummers to encourage an attack and on one occasion a Russian officer with the Vilensky Regiment noted that '… drummers beat the attack…' He also noted how: 'The roar of enemy fire, the doleful scream of shells and sound of them exploding, merged with the roar of firing from our own battery of guns. We were enveloped in smoke…' Such noise drowned out the sound of the drum beats, although the bugle, with its own distinctive sound which at one time had been the drum's uniqueness on the battlefield, was now the rallying signal for troops. Although the rank of drummer was still being used as a title, the bugle was just as likely to be carried in place of the drum. For example, on the night of 19–20 April 1855, the 77th Regiment of Foot (later to become the Middlesex Regiment) undertook a night attack against a Russian position, during the course of which 15-year-old Drummer MacGill, orderly bugler to Colonel Egerton, entered a Russian trench and captured a Russian bugler. The Crimean War added another 'first' to its list by being the first conflict where more men died through disease than enemy action. After the war, many French and British regiments would paint the battle honours of such engagements as Inkerman, Sebastopol and Alma to the list of those other battle honours already adorning the side drums carried by their respective corps of drums.

The Crimean War had not long been over when the British army was put to the test again on the other side of the world, when the uprising known as 'The Indian Mutiny' erupted in May 1857. The British army would not be involved in any European wars for another sixty years, but it was kept busy in other parts of the world such as South Africa and India, which were part of the British Empire. This included the Indian Mutiny, the Zulu Wars in 1879 and conflicts in a dozen other countries around the world. In Europe, France and Austria went to war against each other in 1859, and so great was the casualty rate in this fierce war at battles such as Solferino and Magenta that it led to the establishment of the International Red Cross in 1864. In 1866, war broke out between Austria and Prussia and four years later, from 1870–1871, France and Prussia fought a war, which brought about the end of the rule of Napoleon III. Such large-scale wars and even the many other relatively minor campaigns continued to bring about a change in the course of warfare which had one fundamental theme connecting them: the railways.

Steam engines had been used for a number of purposes for many years to pump water from mine shafts and even to operate lifting gear such as cranes. Small locomotives had been used to haul heavy loads at quarries and coal mines. By 1830 the first commercial railway in the world was opened in Britain when the Liverpool and Manchester Railway was established between the two industrial cities. It did not take long for the military to recognise the potential and in that same year the British army conducted the first experiment of its kind by moving an entire regiment of troops a distance of 34 miles in only two hours by railway. This accomplishment showed how an army's marching time to cover the distance, which would have taken at least two days full march, was reduced to only a couple of hours. By 1835 other European nations such as Prussia had undertaken the same experiments. In 1839 the Prussians demonstrated its results by moving

8,000 troops by rail between Potsdam and Berlin, a distance of 18 miles. The distance may not have been great, but in the days before railways it would have taken an army at least one and a half days to cover that distance. Railways had once again demonstrated that they could cut mobilisation time down to hours and all the ammunition and supplies, including horses, could be moved as one. In 1846 the Prussians again showed their martial efficiency by moving the entire VI Army, some 12,000 men, by rail. Three years later in 1849 the Russians transported an entire army corps of some 30,000 men between Poland and G'oding in Moravia.

During the Franco-Austrian War of 1859, the French army moved 250,000 troops into Northern Italy in only six weeks. A British commentator recorded two years later that in his opinion: '... railways in close connection with vast military operations would alone be enough to give distinction to this campaign in military history'. At one point in only twelve weeks, between April and July that year, the French moved over 600,000 troops and 129,000 horses by rail. On average they were able to transport almost 8,500 men direct to the theatre of operations, along with over 500 horses, per day. A report appeared in *The Times* newspaper stating how: '... from the heights of Montebello the Austrians beheld a novelty in the art of war. Train after train arrived from Voghera, each train disgorging its hundreds of men and immediately hastening back for more'. Armies were no longer marching into battle with the sound of the beating drum, but rather transported in their thousands to the clatter of the wheels on the steel tracks which had spread out across Europe. From no railway tracks at all in Europe in 1825, there were over 175,000 miles of track laid by 1900 and this network continued to expand. All the while it made it easier and quicker to send an army to war. For example, the distance from Cologne to Rome is approximately 1,000 miles and before the advent of the railways it would have taken an army ten weeks of marching to cover the distance. By 1900 an army and all its supplies could be delivered over the same distance in only twenty-four hours. The troops would be fresh and all the ammunition they required was immediately available to them, with more support arriving continuously as long as the trains operated. Some 200 years earlier, during the Great Northern War, a typical Austrian *cuirassier* (cavalry) regiment had required each man to carry provisions for four days and each of the 150 wagons accompanying the regiment carried provisions for a further twenty-six days. Railways did away with that necessity and meant that supplies could be brought up in vast quantities in one movement.

In 1832 General Lamarque, in a prophetic appraisal of the use of railways, concluded that it was: '... a revolution in military science as great as that which had been brought about by the invention of gunpowder'. On the outbreak of the First World War in August 1914, each of the sixty-two divisions of the French army, eighty-seven divisions of the German army, forty-nine divisions of the Austrian army and 114 divisions of the Russian army, could be moved, in theory at least, by rail. Each division had a unit strength of 15,000, so the French army alone had 930,000 troops to be moved, which would have been almost impossible without trains. The supplies of dried food stocks and fodder for the horses could all be moved by rail along with ammunition and when the trains returned they could transport the wounded back to the hospitals. Drummers for the first time in centuries were surplus to requirement, except for ceremonial parades such as escorting departing troops marching to the railheads for transportation to the field of battle. During the Austro-Prussian War (1866) the entire Prussian Guard Corps was mobilised in only one week, with twelve trains departing each day on a timetable which would show the world the efficiency of the Prussian military war machine, demonstrated again during the Franco-Prussian War (1870–1871) and the First World War. Although the railways were well used in Europe, it was actually on the other side of the Atlantic during the American Civil War that they would come to really show their worth. America in 1860 had almost 31,000 miles of railway track, which represented more than the rest of the world combined to a ratio of 2.4:1 miles.

THE AMERICAN CIVIL WAR

The Franco-Austrian War in Europe had only been finished some eighteen months when the first rumblings of war were being circulated in America. The country was thousands of miles away across the vast Atlantic Ocean, but many émigrés had left Europe and were heading for a new life in America. Most were civilians, but some were former soldiers who had either seen fighting in the Crimean War, the Franco-Austrian War or one of the many other minor wars on the Continent. By April 1861 the first shots had been fired in anger and Fort Sumter had been bombarded before eventually surrendering. The officer class was not entirely without experience of mid-nineteenth-century warfare, but it was limited. Future prominent commanders, such as Captain, later General, George McClellan, were sent as military observers to report on the events of the Crimean War. One of his reports noted how the French *Zouave* troops were: '... [the] most reckless, self-reliant, and complete infantry that Europe can produce'. From such observations on this conflict and other European wars, such as the Franco-Austrian War of 1859, similar reports were compiled in which the authors emphasised the growing use of railways to move troops over vast distances. Indeed, McClellan had participated in the surveys for the first railways being laid in America and his knowledge of this and his appreciation of the importance of railways would come to stand him in good stead. There may have been almost 31,000 miles of railway track across America, but it had been built disproportionately, with over 22,000 miles covering the northern states and barely more than 8,500 miles in the southern states.

Men volunteered as soldiers and the drummer boys caught up in the conflict, later known as the American Civil War (1861–1865), were following in the footsteps of so many young men who had gone before them. Many young boys, often with little or no prior experience in music, joined the armies of their respective sides in their thousands. In the Union Army, it has been estimated that the number of boys joining as drummers, buglers or fife players may have been as high as 100,000. One such recruit was a boy named William Bircher, who tried to enlist in the 2nd Minnesota Infantry Regiment of the Union Army, but at 15 years of age he was considered too small to serve as an infantryman. Disappointed at being turned down, he tried to enlist again and successfully joined the regiment as a drummer. There were boys of all ages in the ranks, both younger and older than Bircher; boys such as Edwin Jennison, 17, who was serving as a drummer in the Confederate Army when he was killed at Malvern Hill in 1862.

The war was fought over distances more vast than anything seen in Europe up to that time. Railways made it possible, but drummers were now passengers on these trains as entire regiments were transported to theatres of operations. For example, in September 1863 the Union Army of the Potomac sent 23,000 troops to support actions in eastern Tennessee. This was accomplished, along with their artillery and horses, in only one week over a distance of 1,200 miles, which would have taken twelve weeks to march on foot. Over a year later, General Schofield's corps of 15,000 men were sent via an extended route of 1,400 miles by rail from Tennessee to Potomac to further show the power of the railways. Throughout the war more tracks would be laid, thereby making the movement of troops easier and faster and ensuring the supply of equipment and reinforcements. The role of the drummer was reduced to the battlefield, now that whole columns of troops did not have to march everywhere. On the battlefield itself, drummers were gradually being replaced by buglers, whose distinctive calls were distinguishable from the sound of gunfire when the beat of the drum was being drowned out by exploding shells. Despite this, drummers were still required to be present for morale purposes, as the troops were used to seeing them and their tapping out of the step to march as they advanced.

The duties of drummers were similar on both sides and daily routine in the opposing armies was almost identical. Drummers had to be among the first to rise in the camp, having been roused by the sentry on duty. And together with the bugler would sound Assembly. At set times during the day they would also beat signals for troops to parade to water horses, drill parades and for mealtimes. Drummers were also used to carry the wounded from the battlefield, dig ditches, sort mail and other menial tasks, and yet still be alert enough to beat 'lights out' across the camp at the end of a working day.

Robert Henry Henderson from Michigan is believed to have been only 10 years old when he enlisted in the Jackson County Rifles as a drummer boy in 1861. Units such as the Bealton Virginia Drum Corps would have boys of all ages, each one eager to 'do his bit'. It may sound strange that boys as young as this were allowed to join the army, but back in Victorian Britain boys the same age as these were joining the army. Their departure from family life may have been a great wrench for the family, but it meant one less mouth to feed and if they could send money home then it could help to feed the other children. The same thing was happening across Europe, from Italy to Spain, and the Austro-Prussian War of 1866 would see young drummer boys marching across the battlefields, keeping step with the older fighting men.

The military career of Robert Henry Henderson is well documented and he is recorded as being 4ft 6in tall at the time of his enlistment as a drummer. He practised his skills often, much to the annoyance of the older men who thought him a 'perfect little pest'. The Jackson County Rifles were sent to Fort Wayne near Detroit where the unit became C Company of the 9th Michigan Infantry. Despite being dismissed for his small size, Robert was determined to stay with his regiment and, using his diminutive size, ducked through the mingling ranks of soldiers as they packed together to entrain for Fredericksburg in 1862. By now aged 11, but probably still not much taller, he was on the field of battle on 13 June at Chattanooga. Apparently he was wounded in the fighting and taken prisoner by the Confederate forces, but later released because of his tender age. Undeterred by his experiences, Robert promptly joined another regiment and further exploits followed and he survived the war. Also known possibly as Hendershot, his later life has come under some scrutiny and certain aspects of it veracity are questionable, the fact remains that his early career did happen and photographic evidence exists to support it.

The American Civil war abounds with other similar stories of drummer boys, such as 13-year-old Johnny Cook, who served with the 4th US Artillery and, at the tender age of 15, was present at the Battle of Antietam on 17 September 1862. Orion Howe, whose age has not been properly determined, served with the 55th Illinois Volunteers as a drummer and was wounded at the siege of Vicksburg. Despite his injuries, Orion continued to carry messages. An un-named drummer serving with the 14th Connecticut Regiment was taken by surprise by three Confederate soldiers as he was filling a pot with water from a stream. Quickly composing himself, he bluffed them out with some smart thinking and called for them to surrender. Probably believing there were other soldiers nearby, the men did as they were told and the boy took them prisoner.

No doubt the most famous drummer boy of the American Civil War was Johnny Clem, who was only 10 years old when the war began and managed to attach himself to the 3rd Ohio Volunteers, his local regiment. He was ignored by regular regiments, but eventually became attached to the 22nd Massachusetts Regiment as a drummer. He was too young to be on official muster lists, so the officers between them donated $13 per month for his keep and a uniform was specially altered for his small size. In September 1863, by now aged 12, he was officially old enough to be a drummer and paid for his services as such. Johnny Clem was present at the Battle of Chickamauga where he is believed to have shot a colonel in the Confederate army. He was captured, but managed to escape and his exploits became known to journalists working for northern newspapers reporting on the war, calling him Johnny Shiloh.

Johnny said his drum had been smashed by a cannon ball during a battle, which is quite possible given the chaos of war. Later, while in transit on a train, he was captured for a second time by Confederate troops, who rebuked the Federal army for sending boys to fight. This was hypocritical because the southern states also used boys as drummers and fighting troops. For example, a boy believed to be around 11 years of age and known as 'Little Oirish' from Kentucky is listed as having served as a drummer with the 1st Kentucky, nicknamed the 'Orphan Brigade'. The Confederate Army was not averse to even using black men from slave-owning families and putting them to work in the role of labourers in digging trenches, earthworks or latrines in the camps. This role dated back to the so-called 'Virginia Code' of 1705 governing the use of slaves in time of war. There were some black drummers who served in the Confederate Army such as Henry Brown, understood to have been a bricklayer and therefore possibly a freeman who enlisted with the Darlington Guards in 1861 and served with the regiment as a drummer. He later served with other units, including the 8th and 21st regiments, and was present at the Second Battle of Manassas on 28–30 August 1862. Brown's actions on the battlefield attracted the attention of General W.E. James, who wrote how: 'He [Brown] was beating all the time regardless of the danger...' He went on to comment: 'He followed on to the battlefield and was under fire with the others'. It could well be that the old soldier Jordan Noble may have assisted in recruiting these black troops to the ranks, having regaled them with old regimental stories. As for Johnny Clem, he was later exchanged for a Confederate prisoner and was assigned to General Thomas's staff, serving as an orderly and messenger until his discharge in September 1864. He had been luckier in his war service than Clarence McKenzie, who served with the Brooklyn 13th Regiment as a drummer aged 12 years old. He was killed at Annapolis and is buried in the Greenwood Cemetery.

After the Civil War, Johnny Clem was nominated by President Grant to attend the West Point Military Academy in recognition of his war service. However, he failed to pass the entrance exam, although President Grant still appointed him to the rank of lieutenant. Johnny continued his service career until 1915, by which time he held the rank of brigadier-general. After he retired from the army he settled in San Antonio, Texas and died in May 1937. He is buried in Arlington Cemetery and his career from drummer boy to brigadier-general is surely unique in the annals of American military history. Another prominent drummer to emerge from the war was Willie Johnson from St Johnsbury in Vermont, who joined D Company of the 3rd Vermont Regiment and served in the Seven Days Battle during the Peninsular campaign and was the only drummer to keep possession of his drum. For this act he was recommended for the Medal of Honor and, on receiving it at the age of 13, was one of the youngest recipients of the award.

Like drummers in other armies of the day, the uniforms worn during the American Civil War were heavily influenced by European armies, such as the French from the time of Napoleon Bonaparte, and were just as flamboyant. The regiments which fought in the conflict included colourful *Zouaves*, hussars, dragoons, lancers and many other terms for fighting units which did not originate in

America. These regiments did not just blossom with the outbreak of war, some, such as the 1st Regiment of Virginia Volunteers, had been raised before the war. In April 1860, the year before war broke out, this regiment had a corps of drums which included sixteen drummer boys, all attesting to being over the age of 16 years old and wearing a uniform of 'red jackets and white pants'. From the description of Drum-Major Charles Rudolph M. von Pohle's uniform, he would not have looked out of place at the head of any corps of drums in Europe, wearing as he did: '… a gray frock coat with black plastron front and gold lace braid linking three rows of ten gilt buttons; gray trousers with gold lace seam strip; red sash trimmed with blue; and tall bearskin cap topped with a large red, white and blue pompom'. It was all very reminiscent of an era long-since passed, except for the last traces which were fading away in Europe. Such grandiose uniforms would only be acceptable on parade grounds for ceremonial occasions and the armies in America would quickly come to realise the same.

Like their counterparts in European armies, the drummers in the American Civil War marched in column while on campaign and joined them on the field of battle to beat out a rhythm to advance at a steady pace. Like so many before them, the prospect of battle was a terrifying thing to contemplate; particularly now, with the devastating effect of musket fire, especially at close range. There was also artillery fire, which used a solid, iron shot, which could tear off a man's leg, and exploding shells which, upon bursting within the enemy ranks, threw out lumps of iron in all directions. This was known as shrapnel and could kill or maim indiscriminately as pieces of the shell flew out and could easily penetrate a soldier's flesh. At closer range, the troops could expect to be fired on by artillery using either canister or grapeshot, each of which was designed for use against massed targets at close range, especially charging cavalry. Canister shot was made of a thin sheet of metal formed into a tube and nailed to a wooden base to form a receptacle, this was then packed with dozens of musket balls and the open end sealed off. This type of ammunition had been in use for many years and had been very effective during the Napoleonic wars. On being fired the thin metal sheet was torn open by the blast of the main charge and the musket balls expended like a gigantic shotgun. Grapeshot comprised of larger iron balls stacked around a central wooden core and held in place by either hessian or netting, so that it resembled a deadly bunch of grapes. Used primarily against cavalry, where the large calibre iron projectiles would bring down the horses, it had been deployed as early as the English Civil War in the seventeenth century. On firing, the hessian covering or netting holding the balls in place was torn away by the blast of the main charge and the many iron projectiles tore their way through the advancing ranks. Into this maelstrom of lead and iron the troops had to advance and the drummers had to go with them.

No wonder, then, that many men sat and reflected on the prospect of what they had to face on a battlefield in an industrialised war. At the five-day Battle of

Fredericksburg, fought from 11 to 15 December 1862, the Confederate Army of
72,500 men and commanded by General Robert E. Lee faced a Federal army of
almost 116,700 Union troops, commanded by Major-brigadieGeneral Ambrose
Burnside. The fighting would see over 13,300 Union troops killed and wounded
for a Confederate loss of some 4,500. At one point in the battle, a Confederate
officer observed: 'The enemy, having deployed, now showed himself across the
crest of the ridge and advanced in columns of brigades, and at once our guns
began their deadly work with shell and solid shot. How beautifully they came on.
Their bright bayonets glistering in the sunlight made the line look like a huge
serpent of blue and steel. The very force of their onset levelled the broad fences
bounding the small fields and gardens that interspersed the plain. We could see
our shells bursting in their ranks, making great gaps; but on they came, as though
they would go straight through and over us. Now we gave them canister, and that
staggered them. A few more paces onwards and the Georgians in the road below
us rose up, and, glancing an instant along their rifle barrels, let loose a storm of
lead into the faces of the advance brigade. This was too much; the column hesi-
tated, and then turning, took refuge behind the bank'. Despite echoing the words
of the Duke of Wellington who commented: 'they came on in the same old way
and we stopped them in the same old way...', there was no alternative, with each
man knowing full well there was no other choice but to advance.

Troops wrote of their feelings before, during and after battle; for example, the
Confederate soldier who wrote, just before the Battle of Shiloh in April 1862,
'I have the shakes badly'. A Union soldier wrote to his family how he had seen
'... men rolling in their own blood' before going on to write: 'They lay mangled
and torn to pieces so that even friends could not tell them'. A Confederate soldier confessed in a letter that he had '... shot men until my heart was sick with
slaughter'. Only after the battle was over there was time to sleep, as one soldier
wrote: '... [I] did not know how tired I was until the excitement of the battle
was over'. Then came the gathering up of the wounded for treatment. This was
the duty of the stretcher bearers, the medical staff and the drummers, who gathered up friend and foe alike and were following in the footsteps of the likes of
Baron Larrey, Napoleon's brilliant surgeon, and the British surgeon of the same
period, Sir Charles Bell. Some of the troops who fought during the Civil War
were European émigrés, many of whom had seen battle before, such as the many
Irishmen and Englishmen who had fought in the Crimean War only a decade
earlier. Some of the French troops serving in the ranks may have seen action
during the Italian Independence Wars and there were many who had military
experience of some sort, even if only during peacetime. It has been opined that
during some battles, perhaps twelve or more different languages may have been
heard, ranging from Spanish, Russian, Prussian, Italian and, of course, English.

Casualties had to be removed from the battle and taken to the doctor for treatment. If a soldier was wounded early in battle, or even before the battle began,

he could find himself probably receiving good treatment. However, as the battle progressed and things became hectic, medical treatment was more basic. The unfortunate wounded had to lie on the battlefield until the engagement was over and he was removed to have his wounds treated or face amputation of an arm or leg. Drummers serving as stretcher bearers had to go onto the battlefield at all stages of the fighting, as evidenced by David Auld, a drummer with the 43rd Ohio Volunteers, who wrote of his experiences at the Battle of Corinth in Mississippi on 30 October 1862. David Auld wrote: 'While watching these battle lines so grand to look upon, but so terrible to think of when you remember the frightful waste of human lives they caused, the call came "Bring the stretchers, a man hurt." Myself and Demas took the stretcher to look for the man, he was pointed out to us and proved to be Bradford (our older brother) who had been struck by a shell in the left shoulder while lying on the ground in line waiting for the first assault just opening. By his side lay James W. Conger whose clothing was stained by his blood. We were little more than children and the shock to us can be imagined better than described. Demas and myself lifted him to the stretcher just as Colonel Kirby Smith and Adjutant Heyl were shot from their horses a few steps away. We carried him to the shallow ditch by the railroad a few rods to the rear, where the temporary field hospital was located, as it offered a slight protection to the wounded from the deadly hail of bullets that fell about them coming from all directions except the rear. We then placed him in an ambulance still alive and conscious.'

The experience would have indeed been harrowing for the young David Auld as he watched men killed around him whilst rescuing his wounded 'brother'. It is unlikely that the man was his brother in the true sense of the term, but rather his 'brother in arms'; nevertheless, it took great fortitude to recover the man. The distance of a 'rod' is approximately 5.5yds or 16ft 6in, but even so, under enemy fire the task would have taken a great deal of effort. Drummer Auld mentions that he was little more than a child and whilst he does not state his age he was probably less than 14 years old. It has been estimated that around 300 drummers in the Union Army may have been as young as 13 years old, but some were even younger, such as Tommy Hubler, aged 9.

The story of Thomas L.F. Hubler is an example of how patriotism affected so many men and young boys who, in generations before and after, wanted to be part of it and do their bit for whatever side they fought on. Tommy was born on 9 October 1851 in Warsaw, Poland and was 2 years old when his family emigrated to America. His father had seen military action and when President Abraham Lincoln put out the call for 75,000 volunteers for the war, he responded. Tommy joined his father's unit, E Company 12th Indiana Infantry Regiment, and served as a drummer at the age of just 9. He served throughout the war, surviving the Maryland and Virginia campaigns, and is understood to have been present at twenty-six battles, making him a true veteran. In later life Tommy returned to his native Warsaw, where he died in 1913 aged around 64.

By the time the American Civil War ended in 1865, the role of the drummer as a signaller was beginning to finally come to an end, as it was in many armies, including the British army. They would still be found in the ranks on occasion, but now the bugler was replacing the drummer, although the term 'Drummer' still survived. The two types of musicians had been parading together for some time and, indeed, some drummers were trained as buglers. With the passing of time, the drum was eventually taken out of frontline campaign service and only used for ceremonial parades, such as officer graduations, Trooping the Colour in London and marching through towns to 'Drum up Support' and attract potential recruits to join the army to fight. The main purpose of the drummer may have disappeared over the centuries, but it had not lost the ability to attract men to the ranks since the days when Captain Blackadder wrote of his experiences as a recruiting officer in 1705.

INTO A NEW ERA

As the nineteenth century progressed, so more images of drummers were circulated in the many popular publications of the day. Artists of earlier times had depicted drummers in their paintings of battle scenes, showing piles of drums stacked to convey the martial air, and this came to represent the classical military image. Artists depicting military events in the nineteenth century included Stanley Wood, W.H Overend and R. Caton Woodville, who produced an image showing drummers advancing at the Battle of Blenheim on 13 August 1704. Lady Butler produced some fine paintings showing images of the Crimean War, the Defence of Rorke's Drift and especially her composition called 'Steady the Drums and Fifes', which showed the drummers of the 57th Regiment of Foot (later to become the Middlesex Regiment) at the Battle of Albuera on 16 May 1811, where the regiment earned for itself the nickname 'The Diehards'. This imagery was later joined by the work of such photographers as Roger Fenton, who took photographs of the Crimean War.

On the night of 26 February 1852, an event occurred which inspired artists to paint a record of the scene, and led to the familiar phrase 'women and children first' when the call came to evacuate due to danger. On 25 February 1842, HM Troopship *Birkenhead* sailed from Simonstown on the last leg of her journey to transport troops to Port Elizabeth as reinforcements to fight in the Second Kaffir War in Natal, southern Africa. Late in the evening, during a fierce storm, the vessel was driven onto a reef of rocks off Cape Danger. On board were 638 men, and women and children, who were assembled on deck as the ship foundered and began to break up. There was no panic and troops performed their tasks to which they were detailed. The troops on board the stricken vessel came from at least ten different regiments, including Colonel Alexander Seton of the 91st Highland Regiment (Argylls) who supervised the transfer of the women and children into the lifeboats. The troops stood firm and accounts from some of the 193 survivors recorded that there was a drummer on deck beating out signals. One survivor stated that: '… there was not a murmer or cry among them [the troops on deck] until the vessel made her final plunge'. It was dramatic heroism and just the stuff for artists such as Thomas M. Hemy who painted the scene, including the young drummer boy. Colonel Seaton died in the wreck, along with 444 others, but the event showed the stoicism of troops in the face of imminent disaster. In Prussia, the emperor ordered the account to be read out before every regiment of the Prussian army as a tribute to those who had lost their lives in the tragedy.

From that time, images of drummers, especially on parade, were to be seen in the popular periodicals around the world. People could now see exact likenesses of the figures they were reading. This included men such as Drummer Flinn of the 64th Regiment of Foot (later to become the North Staffordshire Regiment) who on 28 November 1857, during the Indian Mutiny, won the Victoria Cross for saving the life of a comrade under fire. He was aged just 15 years and 3 months, and is one of the youngest recipients in the history of the illustrious award. It may have been jingoistic reporting in the newspapers, but it was just the stirring stuff the public wanted to read. Readers learned how Flinn was born in Athlone, Ireland in 1842 and enlisted in the British army, before being posted to India as a drummer with the 64th Regiment of Foot. When the Indian Mutiny broke out, the British army had to put down the uprising using great force at engagements such as Cawnpore, where on 28 November 1857 Drummer Flinn, for his '… conspicuous gallantry, in the charge of the Enemy's guns on 28 November 1857, when being wounded, he engaged in a hand to hand encounter [with] two of the Rebel Artillerymen', was awarded the recently instituted Victoria Cross 'For Valour'. Unfortunately, in later life Flinn's character deteriorated and he died penniless in an Athlone workhouse. Another drummer to win the VC during the Indian Mutiny was Miles Ryan, an Irishman from Derry serving with the 1st Bengal European Fusiliers. During the fighting at Delhi on 14 September 1857, ammunition boxes caught fire and some exploded. Sergeant J. McGuire, accompanied by Drummer Ryan, entered the store and threw the burning boxes over the wall into the water, thereby saving the rest of the ammunition and preventing the loss of life it would have caused had it exploded. For their bravery both men were awarded the VC.

The British army of the Victorian period, 1837–1901, was representative of most armies around the world in that it still regarded the role of the drummer to relay signals on the battlefield as very important. After so many centuries of use, the drum and bugle still remained the only truly reliable methods of passing orders to a mass of troops over a distance. However, change was to happen during that time and gradually every army around the world came to recognise that the days of the drummer in frontline service were coming to an end. Even so, there were still plenty of duties for drummers off the battlefield and boys were still recruited into the army. Among the different regiments of the time, the three elite Foot Guards regiments of the Grenadier, Coldstream and Scots Guards were pre-eminent because of their fine fighting traditions, which stretched back to the early seventeenth century. These were formed into the Brigade of Guards and would later be joined by the Irish Guards and Welsh Guards when they were raised in 1900 and 1915 respectively. In 1893, an officer of the Coldstream Guards took pity on a young orphan boy, who had been following the battalion near Swindon, and placed him in the care of the Gordon Boys' Home in Croydon, South London, which had been established as an independent children's home in 1881. The young boy, probably aged 3 at the time, was called John Marshall. Whether that was the name given by his family or he was given this name by the officers is not clear. It is known, however, that he went on to display himself to be a 'fine spirited' lad and did well, learning to play the cornet. He later lived with a foster family for a time before leaving to enlist with the 1st Battalion Coldstream Guards, joining the regimental band as a drummer. The older men in the regiment treated him well and he was popular with all ranks. Unfortunately, nothing more is known about the later life of this drummer and there is no mention of him in the Regimental History of the Coldstream Guards. A spokesman for the regiment stated that: '… Drummer Boys were not an unusual occurrence in those days and there is no reason why he should have attracted special attention'. The regimental archivist could not trace John Marshall through the enlistment books and searching the archives of the Gordon Boys' Home only reveals a photograph of a young boy wearing the drummer's uniform of the Coldstream Guards. There is no name on the file and so there is no way of knowing if this is John Marshall. From the evidence gathered, though, it does seem likely this is the boy in question because the chance of two boys from the Gordon Boys' Home joining the Coldstream Guards as a drummer is most unlikely. It is sad to relate that this is one of those tantalising moments in historical research that a blank is drawn in the story, for the time being at least.

John Marshall and other drummers in the British army would have been instructed how to play the drums using an instruction manual called 'The Art of Beating the Drum', which was published in 1810. It was written by Samuel Potter, who also had published another book in the same year entitled 'The Art of Playing the Fife'. Potter was born in 1772 and enlisted with the Coldstream Guards in 1786, aged around 14 years old. His works, written when he was about 38 years old, contained all the instructions necessary for a drummer to be taught the art of beating the drum, including how to stand with the drum on his left hip and how to hold the drum sticks in the correct manner. Five years after the publication of his books he was the head drum-major of the Coldstream Guards and, whilst not a meteoric military career, this was nonetheless as high as he was likely to rise in the ranks at the age of around 43. By the time he died in 1838, aged around 66 years old, Potter had seen his works being accepted as standard manuals for teaching drummers and fifers in regiments throughout the British army, and saw them reprinted many times.

During the Victorian period of the British army, bandsmen were paid and equipped from the regimental 'Music' fund to which all officers subscribed, which often meant that regiments would compete with one another to see who could provide their musicians with the best instruments, uniforms and equipment. In 1824, bandsmen were mustered as soldiers and drew the pay of their equivalent rank in the fighting companies. In 1781 a royal warrant decreed that 'the drums and fifes' should carry short-swords which should have '... scimitar blades...' This reflects the same eastern influences which had affected the drums themselves. Through the second half of the nineteenth century, drummers and bandsmen continued to carry short swords or bayonets, referred to as 'side arms'. These short swords or bayonets were symbolic and formed part of the overall uniform code of dress for drummers; it is still continued to this day and worn on ceremonial parades. Line regiment bandsmen were issued with the 'Sword, drummers, Mk II' usually carried in a black leather scabbard suspended from a white buckskin frog and attached to the waist belt. Some examples were highly decorated with lion-head pommels or the Royal Cypher of the monarch. By the time of the second Boer War (1899–1902), regimental bands had stopped parading in the actual battle area and the drummers and musicians often served in the role of stretcher bearers, except for the buglers who were retained to play those calls necessary for the functioning of the regiment when in action. However, even as stretcher bearers, the drummers continued to wear their short swords and in 1901 a List of Changes issued for the British army stated that all drummers' swords are to be sharpened before going on service. This order may have stemmed from an alleged incident concerning the massacre and mutilation of boy drummers, which was reported to have occurred during the Zulu War of 1879.

By the 1870s the British had had a presence in South Africa for many years, including a military establishment. White Europeans and native tribes had been in contact and although trade did exist between the two cultures, some tribes, such as the Zulus, were extremely militaristic and warlike. The Zulus and British had clashed in 1843 and again in 1877, and it was only a question of time before war broke out between the two once more. The Zulus began to assemble a massive force of warriors, which gave the British cause for concern and in December 1878 they ordered the Zulus to disperse. When they failed to comply with the request, the British forces marched into Zulu territory under the command of Lieutenant-General Lord Chelmsford. The force entered Zululand proper on 11 January 1879. An early victory for the British over a Zulu force of some 6,000 warriors at Nyezane Drift on 22 January led them to believe the campaign would be a one-sided affair, with British troops armed with modern rifles facing Zulu warriors with spears and shields.

Lord Chelmsford had divided his force into 'Columns' and the engagement at Nyezane was only one action that fateful day. Elsewhere on the same day another of Chelmsford's columns, comprising of 1,700 troops at Isandlwana, was attacked by the bulk of the Zulu army of at least 20,000 warriors. What happened over the next few hours was the worst defeat to be inflicted on an industrialised military army by a native force. It even eclipsed the defeat of General George Armstrong Custer, whose command of 215 men was wiped out by native Lakota and Arapaho 'Indians' on 17 June 1876. By sheer weight of numbers the Zulus overwhelmed the British troops and their native contingents, who were either killed or fled for their lives. Included with the hundreds of British troops engaged at Isandlwana were a number of drummers, who by this time were using bugles, rather than the bulky drum, to relay signals. This trend was being copied in other armies around the world, particularly in France and America, but drums still remained in service and were used in conjunction with bugles in some instances. At Isandlwana there were drummers serving with the 1st Battalion, 24th Regiment of Foot (later to become the Royal Regiment of Wales). Among those killed at the engagement were Drummers C. Andrews, W.H. Adams, G. Dibden, T. Reardon and T. Perkins, but these names only represent a handful of the drummers who were present. When the battle scene around the camp site was later investigated and the dead buried, a rumour began to circulate that the Zulus had hung the drummers up on 'butcher's hooks' and mutilated their bodies.

The highly respected historian Ian Knight, who has written a number of acclaimed books on the Zulu Wars, has studied these accounts in detail and refutes the story. The fact that Zulu warriors in battle did not make any distinction between fighting men and non-combatants is widely recognised. In the words of Ian Knight, 'Anyone found among the British forces was by definition an invader, and was considered fair game. And that included any little drummer boys that had taken the Queen's Shilling and wore her red coat'. Although the term 'drummer boy' is used, Ian Knight points out that most of those killed in the action were probably of an average age of 20 or so. One witness to the scene, Sam Jones, serving with the Newcastle Mounted Rifles, claimed to have seen: 'One sight, a most gruesome one, I shall never forget. Two lads, presumably little drummer boys of the 24th Regiment, had been hung up by butcher's hooks, which had been jabbed under the chins, and then disembowelled; all the circumstances pointing to the fact that they had been subject to this inhuman treatment while still alive'. It would have been hard to stem such stories and indeed they were even embellished by others who had not even been near the location. Soldiers in such alien surroundings would have begun to imagine the worst possible fates which awaited them if they fell into the hands of the Zulus.

In his assessment of the claims, Ian Knight states that it is unlikely that the Zulus would have realised the use of butcher's hooks to hang bodies on to mutilate them, and that to have killed the drummer boys in the way claimed '... suggests a considerable sadism that was generally uncharacteristic of Zulu warfare at the time'. The slashing actions of the deep thrusting assegai spears carried by the Zulus would have opened up flesh and uniforms, causing fatal wounds. To an observer, such injuries at first sight would appear to be an example of mutilation, but this was simply the nature of the weapons used by the Zulus and the results of fierce hand to hand fighting. Later in the day, some miles distant, another encounter was being fought between Zulu warriors and the 2nd Battalion, 24th Regiment of Foot at Rorke's Drift. Between 22 and 23 January, the small garrison held out against repeated attacks by Zulu warriors. There were several drummers present at this action, such as Drummer James Keefe of B Company, 2nd Battalion, 24th Regiment of Foot, and Drummers Patrick Hayes and John Meeham. Like their comrades who were killed at Isandlwana, they too were actually serving as buglers. Rorke's Drift was a bitterly fought battle with hand to hand fighting, although this time the outcome was different. Whilst the casualties were high, the garrison held the defences and in the process won eleven Victoria Crosses, the highest award in the British army. Further fighting took place at actions such as Ulundi, but finally the war was concluded in August that year when the Zulu chief Cetshwayo was captured.

Peace in South Africa did not last long and soon the Zulus had been replaced by Boer farmers in 1880, in what is generally recognised as the First Boer War, which ended in April 1881 with the Treaty of Pretoria. It was an uneasy peace and the Second Boer War erupted in October 1899. Many regiments of the British army served there during the two and a half years of fighting, including units from Australia. This was also the time when, as a military historian has put it, there were to be: 'No more line of battle solid ranks, no more volley-fire and scarlet and gold. [It was in effect] … the end of an era when the commander could watch the progress of a battle with his own eyes'. In 1902 the British army introduced Khaki, a native Urdu term to mean dusty, as the service dress for general wear. This drab, brownish coloured uniform was worn on campaign, relegating the scarlet tunic for ceremonial parades and guard duties. Other armies also introduced an 'olive-coloured' uniform and in Germany the field grey uniform was adopted. The days of the bright reds and blues on the battlefield, reminiscent more of a Gilbert and Sullivan operetta than a modern army, was coming to an end, although some countries such as France and Belgium clung on to tradition with the 'L'horizon bleu' uniform, red pantaloons and kepi headgear. But eventually they too would come to realise that uniforms had to change. Drummers also had to adopt the new design of uniform, but they did still manage to retain a sense of their old flamboyant style with 'swallows nests' shoulder attachments to denote their position.

Conflicts were being fought elsewhere, but huge technological advances were influencing the battlefield. For example, the telephone, which allowed for fast and direct communication between commanders and their armies, and airships, which could make reconnaissance flights to relay information about the depth and width of enemy movements across the battlefield. From the heights achieved in these first airships, more could be seen than ever imagined possible from the ground. The telephone was used by the American army during the Spanish-American War of 1898, and also by the British army during the Second Boer War (1899–1902).

It was again used during the Russo-Japanese War (1904–1905) and with its introduction and acceptance into service by the military, it was another reason to finally
remove the drum from the battlefield and regulate the necessity of the bugle as
an instrument for signalling. It would take time for the telephone to spread, but
by the time of the outbreak of the First World War in 1914, its network of wires
had spread across the world, with messages being carried along submarine cables
between Europe and America. The drum was no longer used on the battlefield,
but it still had a role within the military society and at the start of the twentieth century, although it was believed to be consigned to parades and ceremonial
duties, the military would come to need drums in a way never before thought.

DRUMS GO TO SEA

Marines and Sailors

I n the sixteenth century, England had several pre-eminent seamen, such as Sir Walter Raleigh (1552–1618), Admiral Sir John Hawkins (1532-1595 and whose name is sometimes written as Hawkyns) and, of course, Sir Francis Drake (1540–1596; however, there is some discrepancy over the actual year of his birth and some authorities such as the National Maritime Museum at Greenwich in London put it at 1542). All three were daring men, willing to risk all to achieve their aims, especially in conducting the war against Spain at sea. During this period, France, Spain, Portugal, England and the Dutch were leading European nations at sea, opening up trade routes and exploration. Naturally, this, along with the age-old issue of religion, brought the countries into dispute and sometimes led to war.

In 1588 the greatest threat to England came in the form of a massive Armada of ships from Catholic Spain, intent on invading Protestant England, then ruled by Queen Elizabeth I. Drake has become indelibly associated with the action, but the English fleet which put to sea was under the overall command of Lord Howard of Effingham. The approach of the Spanish Armada into the English Channel was signalled by a series of beacons being lit along the south coast of England, running from Cornwall in the west towards the Isle of Wight and beyond. The defeat of the Spanish fleet did not come about by a single action, but rather a series of engagements and storms which put an end to any aspiration Spain may have had to invade England. Drake's adventures continued to enthral the population and his reputation was enhanced to the degree that he became a legend in his own lifetime. On his voyage between 1577 and 1580, Drake succeeded in circumnavigating the world, carrying with him among his personal effects an ordinary wooden drum decorated with his coat of arms. Shortly before he died in 1596, he ordered that the drum be taken to Buckland Abbey, near Yelverton in Devon, where it still hangs to this day in the care of the National Trust. Over the years, a whole mystique surrounding the drum has been built up, including the legend that if ever England was in danger again, the beat of the drum would cause Drake to return to help the country in its hour of need. The legend was reinforced with the publication of 'Drake's Drum', a poem by Sir Henry Newbolt, which appeared in 1897.

Take my drum to England, hand it by the shore,
Strike it when your powder's running low,
If the Dons sight Devon I'll quit the part of Heaven
An' drum them up the Channel as we drummed them long ago.

Indeed, over the centuries there were some who claimed to have heard the drum mysteriously being beat. One occasion was when the Mayflower departed for America with the 'Pilgrim Fathers' in 1620; another when Admiral Lord Nelson was made a 'Freeman' of the city of Plymouth; and also when Napoleon Bonaparte anchored off Plymouth harbour whilst on his way into exile on St Helena, following his defeat at the Battle of Waterloo in 1815 and subsequent abdication.

When the German High Seas Fleet surrendered in 1918 at the end of the First World War, the crew of HMS *Royal Oak* reported hearing a drum beat. The huge battleship was thoroughly searched, but neither a drum nor drummer was found. In the end, the phenomenon was put down to the legend of Drake's Drum and another myth was added to the history of the Royal Navy. Again, in 1940, during the evacuation of the British Expeditionary Force at Dunkirk, some claim to have heard the drum being beat. Finally, when the city of Plymouth was bombed by German aircraft in March 1941, Drake's Drum had been moved outside the city walls in 1938 to Buckfast Abbey, following a fire at its original home at Buckland Abbey. Some people were reminded of the legend, which said that: 'If Drake's Drum should be removed from its rightful home, the city will fall'. The drum was returned and although Plymouth continued to be bombed sporadically right up until 1944, it survived the attacks. Coincidence perhaps, but the decision to return Drake's Drum was a marvellous boost to the morale of the citizens of Plymouth. The echoes of its phantom drum beat must surely also be added to the spectral sounds of the ghostly drummer at Edinburgh Castle in Scotland.

Europe was not the only region in the world where naval engagements between two strong military states were taking place. At the same time as Drake and his fellow seamen were at the height of their careers, Korea and Japan were locked in war on the other side of the world, as the island-based nation of Japan sought to invade Korea. This was not the first time Japan had been threatened from Korean shores. In 1280 Mongol forces of Kublai Khan had attempted to invade Japan, but his fleet was destroyed in a great storm which the Japanese called 'Kamikaze' (Divine Wind) thus ending the Mongol campaign from Korea. It is believed that drums were unknown in Japan at around this time and that subsequent contact with Korean and Chinese forces in battle may have led to the introduction of drums, which could only be reached by sea. Signalling between vessels was done using flags, as in the armies, and drums were used on board vessels to signal other vessels, the crews or to stimulate morale in battle. If this means of introducing drums into the Japanese military is correct, then it mirrors the way in which drums were introduced into Europe by Crusaders returning by sea. When the *Mary Rose* sank in 1545 with all hands in the Solent waterway, it became covered in silt, which entombed the vessel and all its contents, including personal artefacts, weapons and musical instruments. There it lay for 437 years, until lifted in 1982, revealing a great deal about the Royal Navy in the Tudor period. The *Mary Rose* had long been known about by divers, who surveyed the wreck site and undertook the archaeological recovery of items including plates, shoes and musical instruments, including fragments which were pieced together to reveal a drum known as a *tabor*. This was a double-ended drum which was beaten using sticks and could be used for either marching or as a means of signalling the crew of the ship to various tasks. There were thousands of other artefacts recovered and today this restoration works continues in Portsmouth, alongside the HMS *Victory* of Admiral Lord Nelson.

More than 2,000 years before the legend of Drake's Drum, the crews of Greek warships were serving as oarsmen on vessels known as a *trireme*. In around 500BC, these massive warships, some of which may have measured over 120ft long and 20ft wide, may have been served by crews of over 200 men, of which it has been calculated around 170 would have been serving as oarsmen. Contrary to popular belief, these men were almost certainly hired for this duty and were paid a wage for their services. The crew was well trained and the running of the vessel was orderly, as a warship had to maintain fighting efficiency at all times. The rowers too would have served as fighting men had there been a need for them to do so during battle. It has been opined that it was unlikely that slaves would have been used entirely because during the course of fighting the slaves would have been left unguarded and could either escape or stop rowing, severely compromising the fighting ability of the vessel.

In the later period, Roman galleys also had oarsmen and although some sources claim they kept the strokes by beat of drum, it could just as well have been by chanting or singing. These men were probably not slaves either, unless there was a manpower shortage. Both Greek and Roman military societies had their marine detachments serving on board ship, with archers designated to shoot at commanders and other archers. Over 3,000 years later, their nineteenth-century counterparts were still doing the same thing using muskets. Modern trials conducted by respected authorities such as the Trireme Trust, which built a sea-going replica *trireme* vessel in the 1990s, tried to row in time to the beat of a drum, but it was shown to be virtually impossible. In view of this experiment, the old-fashioned notions of slaves rowing by beat of drum was disproved and the opinion now held is that the crew may have chanted songs or tunes to help keep a rhythm in a similar way that a column of soldiers on the march sang for morale and to take one's mind off the monotony of the task. Flutes and drummers known as *auletes* may also have accompanied the oarsmen on some vessels, but wooden mallets being pounded on a drum or heavy block of wood is almost certainly more of a Hollywood impression than based on any real historical evidence. Drums were used at sea, but it is believed that they were primarily used for signalling from one vessel to another, where the sound was used as some kind of navigational aid to tell other ships where it was, especially in low light conditions. The Egyptians may have used drums in a ceremonial role for royal barges conveying the Pharaoh on the Nile River, where oarsmen rowed at a more leisurely pace, as opposed to battle where speed and power for manoeuvring was required. There are references to drums being used on ships at the time of the Crusades in the twelfth century, but again these would have been for signalling to other vessels and for navigation purposes. The role of the drum at sea would change dramatically during the seventeenth century and remain in use on board warships for over 200 years.

On 28 October 1664 it was recorded how drums were beaten to attract the attention of potential recruits when the Duke of York's and Albany's Maritime Regiment of Foot, the Admiral's Regiment, was being raised. This regiment eventually became the Royal Marines and today they maintain a corps of drums which enjoys a worldwide reputation for the excellence of its performances at public displays, such as the annual Edinburgh Tattoo in Scotland. The occasion was at the behest of King Charles II and with it he established the first modern regular force of naval infantry, beginning an association with the Royal Navy which continues to this day. The order-in-council concerning the raising of the regiment on that auspicious day was issued as: '... twelve hundred men are to be put into one Regiment under one Colonel, one Lieutenant-Colonel and one Sergeant-Major and to be divided into six companies, each company to consist of two hundred soldiers; and to have one captain, one lieutenant, one Ensign, one Drummer, four sergeants and four corporals...' At the Battle of Trafalgar, 241 years later and the greatest naval battle of its day, Royal Marine drummers were to be found on every single one of the thirty-three ships under Nelson's command. The same applied to the forty ships in the Franco-Spanish fleet. It would not be for another fifty years that the bugle would begin to replace the drum as the means of signalling aboard ship.

The Dutch would follow the British example and raise a marine regiment in 1665, with the Russians following suit in 1705. The United States Marine Corps of today can trace its origins back to 1775, when they saw action during the American War of Independence. One of the duties in which the marines were to be used was in the provost role, helping to maintain order and discipline, and to put down mutiny on board ship. Flogging was a punishment used in the navy, as it was in the army, and the sentence to be flogged was given for such serious offences as mutiny or striking an officer. Whereas in the army drummers administered the punishment, at sea it was the 'bosun' or boatswain's mate who flogged the victim using the 'cat-o'-nine-tails'. The punishment was carried out on board ship, with the man tied to a grating and the crew called to watch the punishment, the drummer sounding the order to muster. In the Royal Navy a man could be sentenced to any number of lashes and in exceptional cases, where a courts martial had awarded an extremely high number of lashes for striking an officer or mutiny, the man would be ordered to be 'flogged round the fleet'. This meant that the punishment would be completed in front of each vessel at anchor, with the number of lashes being divided between them. For example, if a man was to receive 1,000 lashes and there were five vessels at anchor, he would receive 200 lashes in view of each ship. The victim would be tied to a grating in a ship's boat and rowed out to each vessel in turn, with a drummer standing in the bows to beat out the signal that they were approaching. On each ship the drummer would beat the signal to assemble and as the sentence was carried out the drummers would beat the 'Rogue's March'. It was a brutal punishment and there are accounts of men dying during its administration. If a man did die, his body continued to be flogged around the fleet until sentence had been completed.

In his works 'An Accidence for Young Sea-Men' and 'The Sea-Man's Grammar', published in 1626 and 1627 respectively, the author Captain John Smith tells how aboard ship, crews were alerted to take station when going into battle by '… sound of drums and trumpets, and [shouts of] St George for England…' Drummers were also used to signal the change of watch as the lookouts were replaced in their duties. The signalling of crews to prepare for battle is known by various terms in the different navies around the world, but is sometimes referred to as the 'Beat to Quarters' in British navy parlance. In the modern-day British Royal Navy it is called 'Action Stations', while in the United States navy it is 'General Quarters'. The French navy refers to the signal as '*Aux Poste de Combat*' (To posts of combat), the Spanish term is '*Zafarrancho de Combate*' (Prepare stations to combat), the German navy call it '*Gefechtsstationen*' (Combat stations) and the Dutch term is '*Gevechtswacht*' (Combatants to stations). On hearing the signal the ship's crew would stow all their kit and prepare the guns for firing. Drums would continue to be used for this purpose until the middle of the nineteenth century, after which bugles replaced the drummer's role.

In all ships at that time, preparation for battle was conducted in a similar manner. On hearing the drums signal the gun crews would attend to their weapons by casting them loose, that is to say untie them from having been secured during sailing time, and they would be checked thoroughly to see they were ready for battle. The crew would strip to the waist, they preferred to work bare-footed, and the decks would have a covering of sand applied to prevent slipping when the blood spilled onto the wooden decks from the wounded men.

The magazines were opened and the surgeons prepared their instruments to set about their task of treating the wounded. All unnecessary items such as empty water barrels would be jettisoned overboard. In some cases the animals, such as cows and pigs carried for fresh meat, were thrown overboard to prevent them running amok during the battle and adding to the confusion. The same pre-battle preparations were practised onboard British, French, Dutch and Spanish ships during this period.

At sea, as on land, it was the drummer who beat out the signal 'call to stations' to assemble the crew for parades or to witness a flogging. However, at sea it was a marine drummer who beat out the call. In Royal Navy slang, the term for a Royal Marine drummer developed into the nickname 'Sticks', as in drum sticks. One of the most popular parades, if not the most eagerly anticipated and popular of all, was the signal to 'up spirits', when an issue of 'grog' (a diluted mixture of rum and water) was issued to the crew. In the case of the Royal Navy it was issued by the bosun's mate and sometimes accompanied by the tune of 'Nancy Dawson', played by the fifes and drums on board. The crew of a warship in the Royal Navy during the wars of the eighteenth and nineteenth centuries could expect to receive a monetary payment on capturing an enemy vessel, equal to a percentage of its value, and this was divided from the captain down to the cook and ordinary seamen. Naturally, the officers received the largest share according to their rank, but even the lowest ratings might receive a few pounds if they were lucky. Records tell that even the Marine drummers of the Admiral's Regiment serving on board were eligible for such payments. Marine Drummer Caleb Gill serving on HMS *Monmouth* would have received such payment of prize money, and when he transferred to HMS *Dragon* he continued to be eligible for the award of prize money, along with fellow marine drummers Jacob Whittingham, William Read and Richard Hopkins, who are all listed on the ship's crew.

Sometimes there was not always enough Royal Marines to spare to serve on ships of the Royal Navy and in such cases infantry regiments were detailed to serve in their place. It is not often that an infantry regiment gets the opportunity to make a contribution to a naval battle, but that is precisely what happened in January 1793 when the 1st Battalion, 29th Regiment of Foot was ordered to leave Windsor in Berkshire and march to Hilsea near Portsmouth to join various ships. They had been chosen to serve aboard the ships because there were not enough Royal Marines available to serve on the British Channel Fleet under the command of Admiral Earl Howe. One unit of seventy-eight men, commanded by Captain Alexander Saunders, was ordered to board the 74-gun HMS *Brunswick*, commanded by Captain Harvey. During one patrol along the Channel, which was aiming to intercept ships blocking supplies destined for Revolutionary France from America, the fleet encountered a force of French ships on 1 June 1794.

The fighting involved cannon fire and the infantry of the 29th Regiment firing muskets in the role normally undertaken by Royal Marines. They targeted and took a heavy toll on enemy officers, helmsmen and the drummers relaying signals to other French ships. The ships of both sides came alongside one another and fierce close-quarter fighting developed. Amid all this carnage, one of the famous black drummers of the 29th Regiment stood proud on the deck of the *Brunswick* and beat out the newly composed tune 'Hearts of Oak' on his drum. Eventually, after four hours fighting, the two sides broke away and the British Channel Fleet had gained a decisive victory at the Battle of Ushant, which is more commonly known in the Royal Navy as the 'Glorious First of June'. The 29th Regiment was awarded the Naval Crown in honour of the part it played in the action and this was appended to the Regimental Colours when on parade. The regiment was also allowed to adopt the tune 'Hearts of Oak' as the regimental 'assembly march' in commemoration of the action.

Fighting also occurred at sea in 1812 during the war between Britain and America. Following one particular engagement, Samuel Leech, who had served aboard HMS *Macedonian*, wrote of his experiences during the battle against the American frigate USS *United States*. On sighting the enemy ship, Leech wrote how: 'The drum and fife beat to quarters; bulk-heads were knocked away; the guns released from their confinement...' This description tells us that the drum beats were known to all the crew and that each man set about his task in readiness for battle. Leech continues how during the battle: '... roaring of the cannon could now be heard in all parts of the ship...' Such noise, which would have included the sound of the enemy's guns firing and the impact of heavy iron projectiles smashing against the ship, would surely have drowned out the sound of the drummers' signals. This graphic account tells also of the casualties caused by muskets and cannons at close range; cannon balls ripping off limbs and crushing bodies, and the wounds inflicted by huge splinters of wood thrown off as cannon balls struck the wooden hull of the ship. These pierced deep and could kill a man as well as any musket ball. The *Macedonian* lost the engagement and was captured by the USS *United States* and taken to America as a prize of war. It was a scene acted out in many naval battles during the Napoleonic Wars, including Trafalgar in 1805, and as the guns became ever-more powerful the suffering of the crew in battle increased and the drummer was drowned out in the noise.

Royal Marines were usually quartered on the lower deck with the rest of the ship's crew, the ordinary and able seamen, but they were kept separate from them in the main, with their hammocks being slung in the stern portion. Marines were divided into two watches, the starboard and the larboard, the same as naval ratings. Apart from the drummers, there would be a sizeable number of marines posted to a vessel to serve as 'sharpshooters' to pick off officers and other prominent members of the crew, such as the helmsman steering the vessel, and even the drummer to prevent him relaying signals. In fact it was a French marine firing from the 'top' of *Redoubtable* who shot and mortally wounded Admiral Lord Nelson as he stood on the deck of HMS *Victory*. This was the same warship from where it was recorded that drums were heard beating signals to prepare for action as the two sides closed for battle off Cape Trafalgar, southern Spain, on 21 October 1805. After the incident, it was a Royal Marine sergeant by the name of Secker who is recorded as having carried Nelson below to be treated by the surgeon. Carrying the wounded to the surgeon would have been another duty performed by drummers and perhaps some were even directed to assist in the amputation of limbs by holding the patient still during the operation. There were two Royal Marine drummers serving on HMS *Victory* at the time of the Battle of Trafalgar, Drummers James Berry and James Long, the latter who was killed in the battle. Both were aged around 21 years old and so were not 'boys' in the true sense of the term. The bugler on board was 23-year-old Phineas Beard, who would have helped in sounding out the signals to the crew, including the Royal Marine marksmen also on board. There were Royal Marine drummers on all ships during the battle and even their French counterparts beat out signals on the enemy ships, as heard coming from the *Redoubtable*.

At the closing of the eighteenth century, the British Admiralty accepted into service a method of using flags to communicate signals, which required only twenty-five flags but had a dictionary of over 1,000 words. This method had been devised by Admirals Richard Kempenfelt and Richard Howe between 1776 and 1790, although the system was not adopted until 1799. This method of signalling allowed two of the most famous signals in naval warfare to be communicated around the fleet commanded by Admiral Lord Nelson. The first was signalled at the Battle of Copenhagen on 2 April 1801 when Nelson ordered signal No.16 to be hoisted to 'Engage the enemy more closely'. This was to become almost his unofficial motto in battle. Four years later he ordered the same signal to be hoisted at the Battle of Trafalgar on 21 October 1805, but it was overshadowed by his more famous signal 'England expects that every man will do his duty'. This method of signalling by flags would be improved on, so that by 1855 an international code of signals for maritime use had been established, permitting some 70,000 signals using only eighteen flags. Signalling between two ships was difficult, but on board it was easy for the drummer to beat out an audible signal for all the crew in every quarter of the ship to hear. This would become more difficult as steam-power and the increased calibre and explosive force of the guns made the ships noisier and further drowned out drum beats. The bugler on board warships did manage to remain in service throughout both world wars, but their role was largely due to custom and tradition, as signals by this time could just as easily be passed by means of intercom systems with loud-speakers and the alarm klaxons. The system of signalling using flags called semaphore, from the Greek *sema* meaning sign and *phoros* to mean either bearer or bearing, was adopted by navies around the world and this enabled signals to be passed over short distances. Semaphore was developed into a fairly reliable form of communicating by line of sight between two vessels at sea over distance, providing that the line of sight was not impaired by bad weather. This use of flags at sea was a natural extension of the use of flags for communication on land, as had been used by armies for centuries.

Gradually a system of unique signals based on semaphore was devised to be used by navies around the world, which took into account spellings and language differences. Eventually electrics lamps were introduced to augment the flags and the signals used by these devices were based on the principle of Morse Code, which had been introduced in the mid-nineteenth century. Radio telegraphy would later replace this method before voice radio allowed direct speech to pass orders throughout the ship. Wooden warships may have had limited space, but there was still room for drummers and the lack of heavy machinery meant that signals could be heard, while the introduction of armoured warships, powered by steam turbines, necessitated radical new designs. Space became a premium as the passageways between the decks became narrower, blocked off by heavy, water-tight bulkhead doors to prevent flooding during battle. These confined spaces served to restrict the ease of movement for drummers with their drums and, as with their counterparts on the battlefield in the army, the days of the drummer at sea was to end. It was technology in warship design which had brought about this change, although the association of drummers in naval service is still evident today with the ceremonial parades of the massed bands of the Royal Marines and other marine regiments, and the navy drum bands of various navies around the world. During both world wars, marine drummers, or rather as buglers, served on board all major warships and were present at most major naval engagements, such as the Battle of Jutland (31 May 1916) and the Battle of the River Plate (13 December 1939). During these battles they were used to sound signals by play-ing their bugles, and as stretcher bearers, and were to be counted among the casualties during any battle. For example, by the end of the Second World War the Royal Marines had lost some 225 buglers and bandsmen killed in action, and many more wounded. During their time at sea it had been a proud era for drummers and buglers in navies all around the world, but it was obvious that the changes being introduced meant it was only a question of time before they were no longer required for signalling in battle.

DRUMS IN THE WORLD WARS

1914–1945

Prior to the outbreak of the First World War in 1914, a trumpeter, bugler or drummer of the British army, who had attained his Second Class Certificate of Education and had joined a Guards regiment, was paid 1 shilling and two pence per day, while a similar musician in a line regiment received 1 shilling and one penny per day. This may not sound much, but it was sufficient enough to distinguish the elite status of the Guards. Drummers certainly had to reach a level of playing which was deemed to be a '... tolerable manner.' During the seventeenth century, one observer wrote: 'I know not whether it be to take more wages, or to be lighter laden, or to be further off...' Today we use a similar remark which has been refined to: 'I'm not being paid enough for this this!' Drum-majors were instructed to be mindful of the young drummers in their charge, especially those taken in as orphans or those who were the sons of serving soldiers, as: '... such boys, from being bred in the regiment from their infancy, have a natural affection and attachment to it'. This was certainly the case concerning John Marshall and his association with the Coldstream Guards who had, as all soldiers, whatever rank or duty, an allegiance to his regiment which is considered sacrosanct and is upheld by his comrades in arms. In an earlier age, another 'child of the regiment' by the name of Robert Mason had been born to a father serving in the 23rd Regiment of Foot (later to become the Royal Welch Fusiliers) and his mother who 'followed the regiment'. At the age of 9, Robert joined his father's regiment as a drummer. He was 19 years old when the American War of Independence broke out, which would put his date of birth some time in 1756. Given his background and circumstances, his outlook for the future would have looked bleak, with no real opportunities to look forward to in life other than to join the regiment. In the event he was probably more fortunate than many lads of his age at that time. At 19 years old he had ten years of service to his credit and the fact he was a drummer would indicate he must have been a bright lad. His baptism of fire came during the opening engagements in the Lexington and Concord campaign in April 1775 where he served as a drummer. He was later promoted to the rank of corporal and when the regiment returned to England he eventually rose to the rank of drum-major. He had survived the war in America, although at one time in 1777 it looked as though he might not survive as, for whatever reason, he deserted briefly and on being apprehended was sentenced to be hanged. However, his officer, Captain Lionel Smyth, intervened and had the sentence overturned. Mason had had a lucky escape and, having learned his lesson, kept a good character for the remainder of his military service, as testified by reaching the rank of drum-major.

On the outbreak of the First World War in 1914 the strength of the British army stood at just over 1.3 million men of all services. In November 1918, after the fighting ended, the army had a strength of more than 3.8 million servicemen. The world had never experienced such warfare. During four years of fighting, the Allies had mobilised in excess of 42 million troops, with France raising 8.4 million, the British Empire, including Canada, Australia and India, raising 8.9 million and America going on to mobilise 4.3 million. Russia was one of the first Allied states to declare war against the Central Powers of Germany and Austria and would eventually mobilise some 12 million troops. Military bands 'drummed up interest' during this period and the sound caused young men to rush to the recruiting centres to enlist. Drums had been used in this way before, but never before on such a scale and the troops in armies learned to march to the beat of the drum in basic training in regimental depots. The tune 'British Grenadier' was to be heard all across Britain, with similar tunes of encouragement being played in those countries mobilising for war. To move such numbers of troops speedily required the use of the vast train network in Europe. There was no use trying to march this number of men to the beat of a drum except to head contingents to the railway stations where they were dispatched to the various sectors of the frontline. At the start of the twentieth century, Russia could only manage to send 200 trains per day to its western borders, but by 1910 military exercises had increased this figure to 250 per day. In 1914, Russia showed its true worth by sending 360 trains to the western frontiers to face off Germany and Austria. Unfortunately, as events would later show, this figure could not be exceeded and not even maintained at that level.

It was realised that from the moment war was declared there would be huge numbers of casualties requiring treatment, and in the British army the number of stretcher bearers was set at thirty-two men for every 1,000 fighting men within the Royal Army Medical Corps, but bandsmen and drummers from various battalions would provide additional local support where their regiment was stationed on the battlefield. This is evident in the number of drummers from different regiments awarded the Victoria Cross for rescuing wounded comrades under fire and despite the huge risks to themselves. Each time the VC was awarded, the *London Gazette* carried an official account of the actions leading to the award and this made stirring reading for the British public. On 18 February 1815 the publication carried the following account of Drummer Kenny, whose award of the VC was one of the first to be made during the four years of the conflict. The citation stated that: 'William Kenny, No. 6535, Drummer, 2nd Battalion the Gordon Highlanders. Date of bravery: 23 October 1914, near Ypres, in rescuing wounded men on five occasions under very heavy fire in the most fearless manner, and for twice previously saving machine guns by carrying them out of action. On numerous occasions Drummer Kenny conveyed urgent messages under very dangerous circumstances over fire-swept ground'. The war was only several weeks old at this point and there would be another 633 VCs awarded to all ranks and services by the end of the war, with a fair share of drummers among that number. Drummer Kenny survived the war and died in 1936, but his deeds are today remembered in the regimental museum in Aberdeen in Scotland.

Another drummer to win the VC early on in the war was Drummer Spencer John Bent of the 1st Battalion, East Lancashire Regiment. On the night of 1/2 November 1914, he took command of his unit's position when the officer commanding and the sergeant were shot and killed, along with a number of men. Bent held the position near Le Gheer in Belgium and defended it against German attacks. Only two weeks earlier he had shown his courage when he assisted in bringing up ammunition supplies under enemy fire. However, it was probably for his actions on 3 November when, under fire, he dragged in wounded men who were lying in 'No Man's Land' which led to him being awarded the VC. He survived the war and later rose to the rank of regimental sergeant major, dying in 1977. Drummer Eddie Slaytor was two months off his 17th birthday when he found himself marching across northern France in September 1914 with the 3rd Battalion, Coldstream Guards. Although a drummer by rank, he actually carried a bugle for signalling parades. At Villers-Cotterets he heard the German drummers beating out and buglers sounding signals, although it would not be long before these sounds became a thing of the past as the roar of the enormous artillery barrages drowned them out.

Both Drummer Kenny and Drummer Bent had performed the time-honoured duties of their rank and position by carrying messages and rescuing the wounded. In the case of Kenny, he went one stage further and also saved weapons urgently needed to fight off enemy attacks. Another drummer to win the VC also served with a Highland Regiment, the 2nd Seaforth Highlanders. He was Drummer Walter Potter Ritchie, who stood his ground at Beaumont Hamel on 1 July 1916 on the first day of the Somme offensive, and continuously sounded the call to 'charge' to rally the troops. He also served in the duties of messenger to carry orders, as did other drummers at the time. Ritchie survived the war and was later promoted to drum-major in the regiment. His achievements are also remembered in the regimental museum at Fort George, Inverness-shire, Scotland. Stretcher bearing duties were also performed by the bandsmen of the Royal Marines, a role they performed in various campaigns such as during the landings at Gallipoli in 1915. Bandsmen and drummers serving in the German and Austrian armies also served in the role as stretcher bearers or as messengers, carrying signals and orders for their battalions and continuing in a tradition going back many centuries. Ordinarily, two men would carry a wounded man on a stretcher, but in the thick, clawing mud on the Western Front it sometimes took four or perhaps six men to carry a stretcher. Captain Charles Hudson serving with the 11th Sherwood Foresters remembered the stretcher bearers were 'wonderful people'. He went on to write that '… ours [11th Sherwood Foresters] had been the bandsmen of earlier training days. They were always called to the most dangerous places, where casualties had already taken place, yet there always men ready to volunteer for the job…' There were cases where men had lain out in the mud in 'No Man's Land', that strip of ground dividing the trenches of the opposing armies, for hours or even days before being found and brought in for treatment by stretcher bearers. Many lives were saved, even after the ordeal of being wounded and then suffering from exposure.

The Central Powers, including Germany and Austria-Hungary, mobilised 11 million and 7.8 million servicemen respectively, and together with Turkey some 23 million men would serve during the war. To move this vast number of men took huge resources in the form of trains. Russia's figure of 360 trains daily to the frontline may have sounded impressive, but Germany's efforts dwarfed that figure by dispatching troops on more than 650 trains headed eastwards alone. The trains were running to military timetables and everything else had to be fitted in around this. Once again, the role of the drummer was to escort the battalions marching away to war from their depots to the railway stations. Once at their destination, the troops would disembark from the trains and form up in marching columns, before drummers and regimental bands led them away through villages and towns where the music inspired the onlookers. There was hardly a town or village across the United Kingdom or in Europe which did not experience an army unit marching through its streets, led by the drummers. These men marched to the railway stations to be transported to the ferry ports where they sailed to France. Once they landed in Calais or Boulogne the troops again lined up with the drums and marched through French towns, the music producing cries of joy in support for the Allied forces. The German battalions marched off to the cheering throngs of their countrymen ringing in their ears, but as they marched through the occupied French and Belgian towns and villages they were only met with stares of hatred. Indeed, for many years after the war the local populace detested the sound of martial music, especially the fifes and drums. Typically, such route marches comprised of fifty minutes actual marching, followed by ten minutes rest. An average infantry division of 12,000 men would require 1,000 railway carriages to transport them and their equipment. Trains leaving for the Western Front were often scrawled with messages such as '*Nach Paris*' (to Paris) or '*Nach London*' (to London) chalked on the sides, and trains leaving for the Eastern Front had similar slogans.

The contingents from Guernsey and Jersey had to sail from the Channel Islands to training camps in either England or Ireland and their departure was heralded by bands from the local militia units. The Jersey contingent was sent to County Cork in Ireland to join the 7th Royal Irish Rifles and spend time there training. On its approach march into camp, the Irish regimental band struck up the French national anthem, the *Marseillaise*, in the mistaken belief that the men were French. It was taken in good heart and the mistake was soon remedied.

America entered the war in April 1917 following a series of incidents which forced it to declare war against the Central Powers. Military parades headed down the main streets of the great metropolitan cities where they were played off by marching bands. On reaching Britain they marched to military bands and were greeted rapturously, and, bringing with them a much-needed vitality, they were accompanied by jingoistic songs such as 'Over There' by George M. Cohan, with its lines: 'The boys are coming; The drums rum-tuming everywhere...', all very patriotic and reminiscent of Kipling's verses. The US army also brought with it a new form of transport in the shape of motorised vehicles. These trucks or lorries could move whole battalions straight from the railway depots to the frontline, and by October 1918 had some 30,000 trucks deployed to France to move troops. These soldiers did not have to march very far and there was certainly no need for drummers to march at the head of the columns. The British army had gone to war in 1914 with perhaps as few as eighty trucks, but by 1918 there were almost 122,000 vehicles in service. The French too had made sterling efforts to produce motorised vehicles to carry the troops. During the defence of Verdun in 1916 it has been calculated that every fourteen seconds one truck began its journey along the 38-mile stretch of roadway known to the French as the '*Voie Sacree*' (Sacred Way), transporting troops at a rate never before imagined in the days of 'foot slogging', as marching was referred to by the infantry. An infantry division in the British army comprised 12,000 men, 6,000 horses and over 1,000 wagons, taking up 15 miles of road and taking five hours to pass any point.

During the four years of war, military bands played concerts and escorted battalions as they marched off to war and a fighting front of trench systems which extended from the Swiss border to the French coast in the north. The war became a stalemate. Assaults which were mounted against enemy trenches were met with the deadly storm of firepower produced by modern weapons, particularly the machine-gun. When the British army launched the attack on 1 July 1916, the first day of the Battle of the Somme, it sustained 30,000 killed and wounded, out of a total force of some 66,000 men committed to the battle. A German soldier, Musketier Karl Benk serving with the 169th Regiment wrote: 'When the English started advancing we were very worried; they looked as though they must over-run our trenches. We were surprised to see them walking, we had never seen that before. I could see them everywhere; there were hundreds. The officers were in front. I noticed one of them walking calmly, carrying a walking stick. When we started firing, we just had to load and reload. They went down in their hundreds. You didn't have to aim, we just fired into them. If only they had run, they would have overwhelmed us'. On the Eastern Front, where Russian troops attacked German and Austrian positions, the losses were just as high: in one attack at the Battle of Tannenberg in August 1914 they lost 30,000 men killed and wounded. With artillery barrages lasting for days, the continuous firing of millions of high-explosive shells and with machine-guns firings hundreds of rounds per minute, the modern battlefield was no place for a drummer to try and even attempt to practice his traditional duties. Long gone, now, were the days of pomp and ceremony accompanying troops steadily pacing out across the battlefield.

When the war finally ended in November 1918, there were numerous victory celebrations and parades headed by military bands, and when the war memorials were unveiled the regimental bands were present and the drummer played his bugle to sound 'Last Post' as a tribute to the dead. The commemoration parades at these memorials continue to this day, with 11 November designated as 'Remembrance Day' and dedicated to those who had lost their lives. The defeated troops of the Central Powers did not return home as heroes, but rather to broken homes and a wrecked economy. From this emerged a number of increasingly extreme political movements, with fiery orators convincing the people that the defeat was the result of being 'stabbed in the back' by conspirators at home, rather than a defeat of the army. Foremost among these would emerge Adolf Hitler and his Nazi Party, who would use the image of the drum in ways not seen since the days of Napoleon Bonaparte.

In his book *Mein Kampf* Adolf Hitler stated that: 'The art of propaganda consists precisely in being able to awaken the imagination of the people through an appeal to their feelings, in finding the true psychological form that arrests the attention and appeals to the heart of the masses.' This he was able to achieve through the mass rallies of the Nazi Party where crowds of 100,000 or more would gather to hear his speeches. The pageantry of the occasion was surrounded in all the pomp and ceremonial symbolism which only a militaristic Fascist regime could create. Hitler stated before the Munich People's Court in 1924 that: 'It was not out of modesty that I wanted to become a drummer'. He was not, of course, alluding to his musical ambitions, but rather to his political aims to become the head or leader of the marching columns, which were to come in the same way that a drummer had always marched at the head of an army. Hitler's Third Reich was not the only Fascist state to be established in the 1920s and 1930s. In Italy, Benito Mussolini was established as the '*Duce*' (Leader) in 1922 and he harboured desires to establish a new Italian empire. Italy had been an ally of Britain in the First World War and Benito Mussolini had served in the Italian army. In 1919 he established the '*fasci di combattimento*' (combat groups), which gave rise to the term Fascist, and Mussolini became the first Fascist dictator in 1922. Mass rallies in which he addressed the faithful members of his party to the accompaniment of music and drums were widely reported in the international press. He adopted ancient symbols of the Roman Empire, such as the *Lictore*, which was an axe carried in a sheath of wooden rods. Fascism spread and there were many adherents following it in one form or another.

However, Fascism was never more powerful than in the Nazi regime under Adolf Hitler, where symbolism was taken to new levels with the 'Swastika', and with banners paraded bearing the legend '*Deutschland Erwache*' (Germany Awake). Free-standing kettledrums, mounted on special stands, draped in black banners and bearing the 'Death's Head' symbol, allowed the drummer to play rolls in these dramatic displays. At one such parade in the Congress Hall, known as the 'Consecration of the Flags' in September 1934, the drums were played by a drummer from the SS (*Schutz Staffeln*) in front of an audience of some 6,000 members of the Nazi Party. As he reached his crescendo and the drum roll died away, the Berlin Philharmonic Orchestra took over to play music by German composers such as Beethoven. At stadiums in cities such as Nuremberg, massed rallies were orchestrated for the Nazi Party by men such as Albert Speer, the architect who would also design Hitler's new cities for the future, although these were never built. He would use hundreds of searchlights provided by the army to illuminate the evening's proceedings and thousands of Nazi banners would be paraded. Regimental bands with drummers and columns of marching troops headed by horses with kettledrums would parade through the streets of cities such as Berlin, Munich and Nuremberg. The international press reported on it and the German people were completely taken in by the panoply. Drums had never before been used in the manner, with processions lasting all day and well into the early hours of the morning; it was dramatic and impressive, inspiring the German nation in support of Hitler.

These ceremonies continued even after war broke out in September 1939, following Germany's invasion of Poland. After the surrender of Poland on 6 October 1939, German regimental bands victoriously paraded through the streets. The drummers of the German army wore 'swallows nests' (*Schwalbennester*) on their shoulders in the traditional manner as worn by drummers and bandsmen for centuries. They were detachable accoutrements which fitted the uniform a series of hooks and eyelets on the tunics, such as the Field Service uniform, but not on the greatcoat, and distinguished the man as a musician. In May 1940 the German army turned its attention toward Western Europe, using a new technique in warfare known as the *Blitzkrieg* or 'Lightning War' and defeating the Dutch, French and Belgian armies in only ten weeks. The British army withdrew to the beaches at Dunkirk from where more than 338,000 French, British and Belgian troops were finally evacuated back to England. Some units, such as the Gordon Highlanders and the Wiltshire regiments hid their drums from the advancing Germans to prevent them from being captured as prizes of war and being paraded back in Berlin. These would not be returned for many years in some cases.

It was not long before the victory parades saw the German army marching through the great capital cities of Europe such as Paris, with the drummers heading the parades seen on cinema screens around the world. The military bands gave impromptu concerts in the open air and also performed in theatres for the soldiers, broadcasting the performances for the benefit of the troops in other theatres of the war. These musical interludes were to become familiar across Europe and were even broadcast on the radio as part of the Nazi propaganda under Josef Goebbels, with stations playing such tunes as '*Bomben auf Engeland*', which was obviously about bombing England, and '*Wir fahren gegen Engeland*' which had England as its intended target. Some famous regiments were engaged in playing these songs, including the *Musikkorps der SS-Leibstandarte Adolf Hitler*, which was Hitler's personal bodyguard. At the state funeral of Reinhard Heydrich in 1942, the Nazi Party orchestrated the cortege with all the pomp and ceremony, which included drums and military bands, surrounding the display for a senior SS officer and member of the Nazi Party. In 1944 the Nazi propaganda machine made a more dignified, but no less orchestrated, display at the state funeral of Field Marshal Erwin Rommel. He had been implicated in the plot to kill Hitler in July that year, but because of his reputation as a military commander and his popularity with the ordinary people he was allowed to take poison rather than stand trial. The funeral procession included military bands and drums beating slowly to mark the solemnity of the occasion. Drums had also been included in the funeral cortege of the German President Paul von Hindenburg in 1934, which had been largely orchestrated by the emergent Nazi Party. The sound of German martial music would be heard daily over the next four years until the Allies returned to liberate France and the rest of Europe. The German army even gave band concerts and marched through the streets of the British Channel Islands of St Peter Port in Guernsey and St Helier in Jersey, which would not be liberated until May 1945. Despised as the occupying forces were, these concerts were nevertheless a form of distraction on the islands as their radio sets had been confiscated and they were forbidden from listening to foreign broadcasts. Like Napoleon's armies in the previous century, the German army bands were heard the length of breadth of Europe, and when the end came in 1945 it was a welcome relief for those who had been under Nazi occupation.

The Allies also recognised the effect military bands could have on civilian morale, and concerts were held in public parks in London and other cities, with famous regiments such as the Grenadier or Scots Guards, which had a band and drummers as early as 1716, or the Royal Marines playing popular tunes. Wherever the British army served, there was a regimental band which would also strike up concerts for the troops and provide music for dances to keep up morale. These bands and the drummers of these regiments were now ceremonial in their role, but that was still to prove important for recruiting purposes and on parades through the streets, enabling the troops to march in a smart, orderly manner.

Despite this new role, they still had to accompany their battalions overseas, serving as stretcher bearers and as bandsmen for ceremonial parades, such as marching at the head of columns of troops when parading through newly liberated towns and villages. From the Middle East to the island of Madagascar off the east coast of Africa, the bands of the British army were to be found playing their instruments. After the D-Day landings at Normandy in France on 6 June 1944, the towns welcomed the bands as they approached to announce the Allies had arrived. They replaced the German tunes with the 'quick marches' of famous regiments, including 'British Grenadier', and the bagpipes and drums of the Highland regiments joined in with tunes such as 'Highland Laddie' and 'Blue Bonnet'. When the war ended in May 1945 celebrations were held all over Europe, with military bands participating in the proceedings. Two months later, in July 1945, there was an official victory parade by the Allies through Berlin, with columns of troops and armoured vehicles, and the Royal Marines band corps of drums leading at the head of the parade.

REGIMENTAL CUSTOMS AND BATTLE HONOURS

Over the centuries the military had readily accepted drums into its culture, but it was not long before the traditions and customs surrounding drums were established. This was repeated in almost every army across Europe where tradition was revered. Over time these customs and traditions became strengthened, embellished and added to with each passing campaign or battle in which drummers served. For the most part, such traditions are confined to individual regiments and within the British army such regimental customs and traditions are certainly held very strongly and form part of the history of the regiment. Some stories involving drums, such as the sounds of the ghostly drummer beating at Edinburgh Castle in Scotland, are to be found as part of the history of many castles, along with other, more specific, locations, such as the ghostly drummer of Tadworth in Wiltshire, which dates from around 1661, and at Tewkesbury in Gloucestershire. The spectral drummer at Edinburgh Castle dates back to around 1650, just before it was attacked by Oliver Cromwell. Legend says that it is a headless boy, but no-one has put forward any theory as to the identity of the boy and why he should play his drum there or why he should have been decapitated. Another part of the legend tells that he only plays when the castle is under threat and about to be attacked. Whatever the explanation, the story makes for good business at this popular historical tourist attraction.

Some of the accounts involving drums are certainly stirring and if it were not for the fact that such stories are corroborated then they would be unbelievable; for example, the story of Mary Anne Talbot, who served with the British army as a drummer and disguised her femininity from the male soldiers. Women have been attracted to armies for centuries as camp followers, either as legally married wives or others seeking to earn money as prostitutes. At the Battle of Uhud on 23 March 625AD, women were recorded as having followed the army onto the battlefield where they beat drums to inspire the men. Centuries later some women went one stage further and disguised themselves as men to serve as soldiers. Their cross-dressing could often go undetected for years, until the law of averages saw them being wounded and requiring medical treatment, which is when their sex was discovered. Some were not discovered until killed on the battlefield. In the British army, Phoebe Hessel served with the 5th Regiment of Foot (later the Northumberland Fusiliers), and Hannah Snell served with the Royal Marines. The true sex of James Miranda Barry was not discovered until she died in 1865. Barry was appointed assistant surgeon in 1815, after serving as a hospital assistant in 1813. By 1858, having seen service in the Crimean War, where she argued openly with none other than Florence Nightingale, Barry was appointed inspector-general of the Army Medical Department. During a military career spanning over fifty years, Barry had even fought a duel. In France, Angelique Brulon served in the army, and many women served in regiments disguised as men during the American Civil War, such as Rosetta Wakeman, Sarah Emma Edmonds and Mary Galloway. Indeed it has been estimated that some 250 women may possibly have served in the Confederate Army during the Civil War.

However, none can exceed the strange case of Mary Anne Talbot (1778–1808), who served as a drummer in Flanders in 1793 and later as a seaman on the *Brunswick* where she was wounded in action in 1794 under the name John Taylor. Mary Anne (sometimes written as Mary Ann) was born in London on 2 February 1778 and may have been the illegitimate child of Lord William Talbot, whose name she took. In later life she found herself involved with one Mr Sucker and by 1792, aged around 14 years old, we know that she had been 'sold' to a certain Captain Essex Bowen, who was serving with the 82nd Regiment of Foot (later to become the Prince of Wales's Volunteers and then the South Lancashire Regiment). No doubt using his privilege of rank, Captain Bowen managed to attach Mary Anne to his regiment as his 'footboy', giving her the name John Taylor. When the regiment sailed for Santo Domingo, so did Mary.

In 1793 an Anglo-Austrian force was deployed to serve in Flanders and one of the regiments involved in the campaign was the 82nd Foot, including Captain Bowen. The siege of Velenciennes during the Wars of the French Revolution was fought between 21 and 23 May 1793 and Mary Anne Talbot served as a drummer. During the fighting, Captain Bowen was killed and Mary Anne was wounded. She treated her injuries herself and was thus able to keep her identity secret. However, with her benefactor now dead she would have to find means to support herself. She deserted the army and joined the Royal Navy, serving on HMS *Brunswick*. It is known that she was wounded in action whilst serving aboard the *Brunswick* in 1794 and the action was almost certainly the 'Glorious 1 June', or Battle of Ushant, in which case she may have witnessed the black drummer of the 29th Regiment beating 'Hearts of Oak' on his drum during the battle. Her time spent as a drummer had been but one brief episode in her life and we do not know if she actually did play the drum in an official capacity or whether she was Captain Bowen's secret 'camp comfort'. Hers had been a life of hardship and struggle and after her death in February 1808, a book telling her thrilling life story was published as 'The Life and Surprising Adventures of Mary Anne

Talbot'. During the same campaign, the 14th Regiment of Foot (later to become the Prince of Wales's Own and then the West Yorkshire Regiment) engaged a French regiment at the Battle of Famars in Flanders on 23 May 1793. The French Revolutionary drummers were playing a tune called 'Ca Ira' (meaning 'This Will Be' and is a song from the time of the French Revolution about how aristocrats were hanged from lamp-posts). The French soldiers were singing to the tune when the commanding officer of the 14th Regiment of Foot ordered his own drummers to take up the tune with the encouraging words of: 'Come on lads, we'll break them at their own damned tune'. It worked and to commemorate the event the regiment later used the tune 'Ca Ira' as a regimental march. Later the tune would be banned by Napoleon Bonaparte, but some French regiments continued to play it as a marching tune.

The tune 'Ca Ira' was not the only one to be 'borrowed' from the French and the 31st Regiment of Foot (later to become the East Surrey Regiment) for a time used a tune called 'Bonaparte's March', which had been taught to them by French deserters. Indeed, Napoleon himself encouraged the use of martial music and the use of drums with such marches as 'La Carmagnole'. This tune is in reference to a short jacket worn at the time and is believed to originate from the town of Carmagnola. It is another Revolutionary tune and is about the fate of aristocrats and was usually accompanied by abandoned dancing, the composer is unknown. French drummers beat out a rhythm on the battlefield called the 'pas de charge' for the infantry to keep step by. The British infantry knew the tune well, having heard it many times, and gave it the derogatory nickname of 'old trousers', but the troops also knew and respected their French adversaries and were well aware of their reputation which had been earned in battles stretching across Europe. Despite this, the British knew that with superior firepower and steadfastness amongst the ranks, and their own drummers beating out the commands to 'make ready' to fire, they could break a French infantry assault. It was a question of nerve and if the drummers and officers held fast the infantry line would follow suit.

Some stories are told by old soldiers for the delight of the younger soldiers within regiments and some of these stories revolve around strange cases where sentries have disappeared whilst on sentry duty and were never seen or heard of ever again. For example, there is the case of the ghostly drummer who has been reportedly seen and heard as he roams along the corridors of the military hospital at Tidworth in Wiltshire. These stories are often told to new recruits, especially if they are due to mount guard at a location renowned for its dark and bloody history, such as the Tower of London where the Foot Guards perform public duties and where the guard is mounted in the presence of the corps of drums. One such particular story involving the disappearance of a drummer boy, which is believed to date back to around the end of the eighteenth century, still persists to this day.

Around this time the 19th Regiment of Foot, which had been raised by Francis Luttrell in 1688 at Dunster Castle in Somerset, was billeted at Richmond Castle in Yorkshire and some soldiers occupied themselves in their spare time by exploring the castle and grounds, which date back to 1071. The soldiers had probably heard the story of the legendary tunnel which supposedly connected the castle to Easby Abbey and ran the distance of about 1 mile following the route of the River Swale. The tunnel was believed to have been built during the medieval period and used by abbots and canons to escape during an attack. According to regimental legend, a group of adult soldiers discovered the tunnel and sent a young drummer boy down to investigate, presumably because he was the smallest and could enter the opening. He was told to keep beating his drum as he walked the length of the tunnel and the men would follow the sound. The young, un-named boy was lowered into the tunnel and he set about his task, no doubt urged on by the older men. All appeared to be going well and the men above ground were following the subterranean drum beat as it led them from the castle towards the Market Place and headed toward Frenchgate. It seemed as though the story about the tunnel may have been correct for they were heading in the right direction towards the river and Easby. Suddenly at Easby Woods, a distance of about half a mile from the castle, the sound of the drum stopped. What had happened? There was no way of knowing and no-one was prepared to go down the tunnel to discover what the problem may be. Had the tunnel collapsed killing the boy? Maybe the floor had subsided and the drummer fallen in. The drummer was never seen again, but some have claimed to have heard faint ghostly drumming. It was a mystery and has remained unanswered for well over 200 years, if indeed it is true.

The element of doubt creeps in due to a number of inconsistencies in the story. Firstly, how did the men account for the disappearance of the drummer? Was he reported as a deserter? The commanding officer of the regiment and the drum-major would certainly have to be informed. Today an annual 'Drummer Boy Walk', with a local boy dressed as a drummer, walks the route to commemorate the event and a marker stone has been erected at the alleged spot where the mystery happened. Those who are interested or curious enough to investigate further, the route can be walked by following the signposts. However, the story appears to be completely apocryphal because a spokesperson from the museum has informed the author that no such tunnel has ever been proven to exist and even geophysics, technology to create an impression of underground features, has failed to reveal any trace of a tunnel. Despite this, the story persists and one has to admit that it does make for great regimental history.

The close association with drums does not end there for the 19th Regiment of Foot. During the Crimean War the regiment fought at several actions for which it gained battle honours, including Inkerman and Sebastopol. At the Battle of Alma (20 September 1854), the regiment captured several drums from the Russian Minsk, Vladimir and Borodino regiments. Today, almost 160 years later and although the 19th Foot is now called the Green Howards, five of these drums are still paraded on Alma Day as regimental trophies. Another regiment taking part in the same battle was the 95th Regiment of Foot (later to become the Sherwood Foresters) and they also captured Russian drums. As a result of this, the regimental custom of the 95th Regiment of Foot was to edge its own drums with black and white triangles in the Russian style. Just over three years later on another continent, the 82nd Regiment of Foot (later to become the South Lancashire Regiment) captured a device referred to as the 'Rajah's Bed Post' when the regiment helped seize the city of Lucknow during the Indian Mutiny on 14 November 1857. It was actually a ceremonial staff used by Indian troops, but the drum-major of the 82nd Regiment later carried it on parade as a regimental trophy.

The presentation of a new set of Colours to a regiment is conducted in a ceremonial parade often referred to as a 'Drumhead Service'. This is because drums were sometimes used as temporary or makeshift tables, with the skin or 'head' being used as a working surface. There are many representations depicting drumhead services, such as Queen Victoria presenting Regimental Colours to the 93rd Regiment of Highlanders (later to become the Argyll and Sutherland Highlanders) on 19 August 1871 at a ceremony held in Queen's Park in Edinburgh. The service, also known as 'Piling the Drums' and used when new Regimental Colours are being presented to a battalion, is sometimes overlooked, but it is very much a military ceremony. The drums are stacked or 'piled' in such a way that they represent an extemporised altar in the same way as drums were used as writing surfaces in drumhead services and courts martial . Usually the pile is formed by the side drums being arranged in a circle, the bass drum stacked on the top and laid on its side, and perhaps an extra drum on top to give extra height if needed. The drummers construct the pile by moving to the designated spot and in turn each man places his drum down. Once the pile has been created the new Regimental Colours are draped over it, an army Padre (vicar) consecrates the flag before it was presented. Once the service has been completed the drummers then move forward to recover their instruments. The Regimental Colours that are being replaced are either consigned to the regimental museum or sent to a church or cathedral associated with the regiment, and this is known as 'laying up the Colours'. There are various statues and other monuments featuring drummers, such as the war memorial to the King's Liverpool Regiment in Liverpool, which shows a drummer wearing a typical eighteenth-century uniform, complete with 'swallow's nest' shoulder epaulettes and a mitre-style cap. The war memorial in the city centre of Newcastle-upon-Tyne is entitled 'The Response', created by the artist Sir William Goscombe John, and is a fine tribute to the men of the First World War. It shows soldiers of the Northumberland Fusiliers marching off to war headed by drummers in the uniform of the period and is very evocative.

Over the years drums have acquired a special aura about them, so that every man in a regiment feels an affinity with them and is proud of them. Like the Regimental Colours, the drums are part of the living embodiment of a regiment and the soldiers within a battalion consider the preservation of the drums to be equally important, especially by the members of the corps of drums. For example, during the First World War in the period known as 'the retreat from Mons', August 1914, and as the British army was falling back in the face of an overwhelming German advance, the 1st Battalion, the Berkshire & Hertfordshire Regiment hid their drums in the village of Paturages to prevent them from being captured by the Germans. Five years later, men of the battalion returned to the village and recovered one of the drums intact in 1919 and from that time onwards it was known as the 'Mons Drum' and is positioned on the right rear flank when the escort to the Regimental Colours is on parade.

Over 100 years earlier at the Battle of Arroyo dos Molines on 28 October 1811, the 34th Regiment of Foot (later to become the Border Regiment) captured the drums of the French 34th Infantry Regiment and these were paraded at the annual Arroyo commemorations. Regimental customs are still observed around the presence of drums, but some are sadly no longer recognised as regiments have been amalgamated and regimental customs change. However, the history of these customs has not been lost entirely because the events surrounding them are recorded in the regimental museums. This includes how the drummers of the 9th Regiment of Foot (later to become the Royal Norfolk Regiment) used to wear black braid in commemoration of General Sir John Moore who was killed during fighting at Corunna on 16 January 1809. The 7th Regiment of Foot (later to become the Royal Fusiliers (City of London)) was allowed to parade through the city of London with '… drums beating, colours flying and bayonets fixed…' since 1924 to mark the regiment's association with the city. In the 5th Regiment of Foot (later to become the Royal Northumberland Fusiliers), the drummers wore red and white roses in their caps on St George's Day, 23 April, and a special unique banner, known as the 'Wilhelmstahl' or 'Drummer's Colour', would also be paraded. On St Patrick's Day, 17 March, the corps of drums of the Essex Regiment used to play Irish tunes for 'Reveille' to commemorate the capture of a French 'Eagle' by the 2/44th Regiment of Foot, which later became the Essex Regiment. On St David's Day, 1 March, the officers of the 23rd Regiment of Foot (later to become the Royal Welch Fusiliers) would receive the smallest drummer in the regiment into their mess, riding the regimental goat mascot and led by the drum-major.

On the other side of the Atlantic in South America, while all of Europe was engaged in fighting the Napoleonic Wars, Argentina and Paraguay fought the Battle of Tacuari on 9 March 1811. By European standards it was little more than a skirmish, but for South America it was a landmark as emergent countries fought for either national recognition or independence. From this battle, a story emerged concerning a 12-year-old drummer boy by the name of Pedrito Rios, who was believed to have been born in Uruguay. During one stage in the battle an Argentine army officer, Major Celestino Vidal, was wounded in the eyes whilst leading his men and he became disorientated. Rios, seeing the incident, used his drum to beat a tapping sound for the officer to follow and the attack continued. Unfortunately, the event cannot be substantiated but that did not stop the legend of the 'Tacuari Drummer' from being created. The myth-breakers have recognised the fact that the boy is not mentioned in any official account of the battle. These same critics also say a boy of such youth would not have been on the battlefield nor would he escort an officer. In all of these instances these critics are incorrect. Firstly, it was not uncommon to overlook individuals in reports concerning battles, unless they had engaged in some outstanding act of bravery which drew them to the attention of officers. Secondly, boys of 12 years of age were at that time serving as drummers on campaign in Europe. Indeed, there is mention of one drummer, Jo Brome, who may have been as young as 8 years old, but whether he was large enough or strong enough to actually carry a drum is debatable. Lastly, the young boy was assisting a wounded officer in the completion of his duty and, although of non-combatant status, he was still a member of the army with a duty to help guide the troops forward by the beat of his drum. In memory of the incident, whether it actually happened or not, 200 years later the 1st Regiment of Foot Infantry 'Patricios' in the Argentinian army still keeps the tradition alive by having a young drummer in the regimental band, putting Pedrito Rios alongside other drummer boy legends such André Estienne.

By the time of the Second World War, drums were only used on ceremonial occasions and drill parades, but the history surrounding them continued to make them part of the fabric of any regiment or battalion. When the British garrison on Singapore surrendered to the Japanese in February 1942, the drums of the Cambridge Regiment were hidden away in an out-building of the Goodwood Hotel by Sergeant Kitson and his fellow NCO Sergeant Morgan. After the war it was believed that the drums had been lost, but in 1946 they were handed back to the regiment by Mr Taylor, whose daughter Mary Taylor had found them and arranged for the drums to be sent back to England. As a mark of respect to the memories of the 784 officers and men of the regiment who had died during three and half years in Japanese captivity whilst working as forced labour, it was decided that the drums should no longer be played. This was not the only regiment to secret regimental drums away to prevent them from being captured by the enemy. During the retreat to Dunkirk in 1940 the 2nd Battalion Wiltshire Regiment was forced to leave behind some of their drums because there was simply no room for them. In June, only a few weeks after the evacuation of Dunkirk had been concluded, the father and uncles of 2nd Lieutenant M.H. Chivers, who was serving with the battalion, arranged for a new set of drums to be presented to the regiment to replace those lost at Dunkirk. The Chivers family ran a local building company and the drums subsequently became known as the 'Chivers Drums'. The Wiltshire Regiment later recovered two drums in post-war years and today these can be seen in the regimental museum at the Wardrobe, Salisbury, Wiltshire, where the full story of the lost drums and their subsequent recovery is told in detail. Another regiment forced to leave their drums behind during the retreat was the 14th Battalion. The fate of these was unknown until recently, after the Gordon Highlanders had one of their drums returned to the regimental museum in Aberdeen in November 2010, having been safely kept by a French family for seventy years. This item is on display at the regimental museum at St Lukes, Aberdeen.

Drummers have long shared the privations and hardships experienced on campaigns with other men, and often their great courage and bravery under fire, regardless of their own safety, has saved comrades from the battlefield. For example, Drummer Spencer John Bent of the 1st Battalion, the East Lancashire Regiment was awarded the Victoria Cross on 14 November 1914 for rescuing a wounded comrade whilst under enemy fire at La Gheer. Such actions were recognised by awarding medals for gallantry and in the British army the highest award is the Victoria Cross. Drummers in other armies around the world have been awarded medals such as the Medal of Honor during the American Civil War and the *Croix de Guerre* has been bestowed on French drummers, along with other rewards, since the time of Napoleon Bonaparte.

The Victoria Cross was instituted in February 1856 and all ranks in the army and Royal Navy were eligible for its award, the inscription on the reverse of the medal reading 'For Valour'. Traditionally the VC is cast from the bronze of the breeches of Russian cannons captured at Sebastopol during the Crimean War. With its institution it joined the list of exceptional military awards such as the French *Legion d'Honneur*, created by Napoleon Bonaparte in May 1802, and the Iron Cross established in 1813. The United States of America created the Medal of Honor for the navy and the army by acts of Congress in December 1861 and July 1862 respectively. This award was open to all ranks and, indeed, in 1862 Drummer Willie Johnston of the 3rd Vermont Regiment was one of the first recipients of the award, later to be followed by more drummers in the America Civil War. The first recipients of the VC included officers and other ranks alike, who were paraded in Hyde Park in London and presented with their medals by Queen Victoria. There were strict rules governing the award and in exceptional cases a man could even be stripped of his VC in the event of having committed a serious crime.

One of the first drummers to be awarded the VC was Thomas Flinn, aged 15 years and 3 months, and was one of the youngest recipients to ever be presented with the medal. He was awarded with the medal for his actions during the Indian Mutiny and he was soon followed by other drummers, such as Dudley Stagpoole of the 57th Regiment of Foot (later to become the Middlesex Regiment) who was awarded his VC on 2 October 1863 for rescuing a wounded comrade during the Third Maori War in New Zealand. In doing so he also demonstrated that bandsmen and drummers served as stretcher bearers in battle, carrying wounded men to the surgeon. However, it was one thing to put a man on a stretcher after the battle, but something entirely different to rescue men under fire, such is a soldier's loyalty to his comrades that he will ignore the dangers. Another drummer to win the VC was 27-year-old Michael Magner of the 33rd Regiment of Foot (later to become the Duke of Wellington's Regiment). On 13 April 1868 in modern-day Ethiopia the regiment was participating in the Abyssinian Expedition and engaged in attacking enemy positions at Magdala. For his part in helping to force an entry through the gates Magner, he was awarded the VC. Born in Fermanagh, Ireland, Magner survived his experience and died in Australia 1897 aged around 56 years.

As well as establishing the VC, the Crimean War also led to some unusual traditions becoming part of the British army. For example, the Black Watch holds a regimental custom on the fifteenth day of each month when the 'Pipes and Drums' assemble to play a piece of music called the 'Crimean Long *Reveille*', which involves a series of tunes such as 'Miss Girdle' and 'Johnnie Cope'. As the name of the tradition implies, it dates back to the Crimean War around 1854 when the pipers played a series of random tunes on their bagpipes to alert the Highland Brigade of a Russian attack. Another explanation as to its origins is that it is a form of punishment for the Pipes and Drums, when a piper, who was the worse for drink, woke the battalion with his drunken playing in the early hours one morning. This typical military humour is to be found the world over, but never more so than in the British army. During a goodwill tour in South Africa in the 1930s, the regimental band of the Gordon Highlanders adopted a dog called 'Champ', who became enrolled as an unofficial mascot. With thirty-nine concerts played in the space of four weeks the dog apparently developed '… an ear for music and likes the bagpipes…' Animals learn to adapt very quickly and even associate sounds with certain things. So it was with Champ, who allegedly learned to recognise the drum roll when the band started to play the National Anthem. It is not entirely clear how the animal expressed this recognition, but the band become so attached to the dog that it was allowed to bring Champ back to Britain. The names of many major battles from the war were also added to the drums as honours to go alongside other historical engagements dating to before the Napoleonic Wars.

Many countries have some form of parade to commemorate a special occasion in the country's history, such as France where '*La Fete Nationale*', referred to as 'Bastille Day', is a national holiday commemorated on 14 July every year and is celebrated in Paris, where the event originally took place in 1789. Others commemorate their independence or liberation and celebrate the occasion with a parade by the country's military, marching in review and accompanied by the massed bands and corps of drums playing martial music appropriate to the ceremonial parade. For example, 'Beating Retreat' is one such ceremony performed today by various regimental bands and corps of drums around the world, and in doing so is maintaining the link to the ceremony's military origins. Few people watching these displays realise that the ceremony dates from centuries ago when drummers would beat out the signal for the troops of opposing sides on the battlefield to withdraw from engagement as night was approaching and the fighting could not be co-ordinated cohesively. The signal to beat the retreat was later used when the gates of walled towns were being secured for the night and was nothing to do with signalling troops to retreat on the battlefield. Typically, Beating Retreat was performed: 'Half an hour before the Gates are to be shut, which is generally at the setting of the sun… The Drummers of the Port Guard are to go upon the Ramparts and to beat a 'Retreat' to give notice to those out with that the gates are to be shut… As soon as the Drummers have finished the 'Retreat', which they should do in less than a quarter of one hour, the Officer must order the Barriers and Gates to be shut'. The ceremony can certainly be traced back to the sixteenth century and it may possibly be even older in some societies. In 1694 an order was issued by King William III of England, which commanded that: 'The Drum-Major and Drummers of the Regiment which gives the Captain of the Main Guard are to beat the Retreat through the large street, or as may be ordered. They are to be answered by all the Drummers of the guards, and by four Drummers of each Regiment in their respective quarters'. As the time of sunset changed slightly every night, so the timing of Beating Retreat also changed, so that by the end of a month, for example, it could have moved either earlier or later depending on the time of the year. Beating Retreat also applied to troops ordering them to return to camp. It remains as a ceremonial parade today and is performed in front of public audiences in countries as diverse as Australia, India and America. In Britain the Royal Marines and the Guards Regiments are perhaps the most famous exponents of the display, but so too are some of the Scottish Highland regiments such as the Argyll & Sutherland Highlanders, whose displays of 'Beating Retreat' at the annual Edinburgh Tattoo are famous the world over.

The ceremonial parade known as Trooping the Colour is unarguably associated with the Household Division of the British army, comprising of the five regiments of Foot Guards: Grenadier, Coldstream, Scots, Irish and Welsh, along with the mounted regiments of the Life Guards and the Blues & Royals, which form the Household Cavalry. Held in London on Horse Guards Parade it is an annual event attended by members of the Royal Household to mark the sovereign's official birthday. It is a public spectacle and also broadcast on television around the world. It is a traditional display dating back in its present form to around 1748, during the reign of King George II, but even after more than 250 years the parade still retains all its pageantry and ceremony. The parade is always attended by the reigning monarch, who inspects the assembled troops and the massed bands of the Guards regiments, sometimes up to 400 musicians provide the music for the occasion.

The ceremony of Trooping the Colour probably dates back to the seventeenth century and perhaps even earlier from a time when the Colours or flags of regiments were paraded on the battlefield as a point where troops would assembly. The Colours are the identity of the regiment, and the motifs and symbols emblazoned on them tell the history of the regiment, especially in the names of battle honours where the unit has fought with exemplary courage. For such distinction in battle the regiment is allowed to put the name of the battle on its Colours and on the drums. Each year a different regiment of the Household Division parades its Colours at the ceremony in London. All regiments in all armies around the world revere their Colours and in previous centuries, when they were taken into battle, it was considered a disgrace to lose them. Indeed, men would go to great lengths to protect their Regimental Colours. For example, at the Battle of Albuera on 16 May 1811, the 3rd Regiment of Foot (later to become the Royal East Kent Regiment or 'The Buffs') fought a hard action, losing 643 killed and wounded out of 740 men. During the battle a French hussar killed Ensign Walsh, who was holding the King's Colours, and he tried to seize them, no doubt thinking what a fine trophy they would make. If he took them he had taken the identity of the regiment. Lieutenant Matthew Latham saw what had happened and picked up the Colours, using the staff to defend against the rain of sword blows being directed by the hussar. Latham ripped the Colours from the staff and thrust them into his tunic, all the while being struck by the rider's sword, which severed his right arm. He was found after the battle still holding the Colours he had so valiantly defended. Lieutenant Latham survived his ordeal, was treated for his injuries and was presented with a gold medal by his fellow officers as a mark of respect for his brave actions.

During the First Afghan War in 1842, Lieutenant Souter of the 44th Regiment of Foot (later to become the Essex Regiment) performed a similar act in saving the Colours by hiding them under his tunic. In 1879 during the Zulu Wars in South Africa, subalterns Coghill and Melvill lost their lives saving the Queen's Colours of the 1st/24th Regiment after the massacre at Isandlwana, and for their actions were awarded posthumous Victoria Crosses. Such, then, is the lengths to which men have gone in order to prevent their Regimental Colours from being captured. Today's Trooping the Colour is a reminder of those days, although is now purely ceremonial. The Regimental Colours are also carried when regiments perform public duties, which includes mounting sentry duty at the royal palaces in London, including Buckingham Palace, St James's Palace and the Tower of London. These duties are sometimes called 'Changing the Guard' and is a ceremony also undertaken at Windsor Castle in Berkshire, where the Ceremony of the Garter is held with massed bands on the Monday after the Trooping of the Colour.

During the parade, and to the accompaniment of the tunes of regimental marches, the infantry march past in slow and quick time, with the mounted regiments also riding past in review. Trooping the Colour is an exhausting ceremony, especially for the musicians and drummers who not only have to endure the physical exertion, but also keep the wits about them and remain mentally alert for the drill movements, especially the 'Spinwheel'. This manoeuvre is performed at one point in the ceremony and entails all the musicians marching in an anticlockwise spiral through 90 degrees. Led by the drum-majors, the movement of the Spinwheel is so complicated that it is not written in any drill manual and is unique to the Trooping the Colour in London. To see 400 bandsmen and drummers moving in such a manner is to witness some of the finest marching skills in the world. The musicians never falter, never collide and keep playing throughout the entire movement. It has been said that the Spinwheel's 'complexity defies description'. If imitation is the sincerest form of flattery then the other countries around the world where similar Trooping the Colour ceremonies are held, such as Australia, Canada, Malaysia and Thailand, are certainly paying tribute to the British army and in particular the Guards Regiments of the Household Division.

Drums and other instruments such as trumpets, bugles or fifes were traditionally played together at ceremonies, but over the course of time the drum is more usually associated with infantry regiments. However, mounted regiments had a need for drummers in ceremonial parades and gradually cavalry regiments replaced some trumpeters with mounted drummers and the foot regiments adopted the bass drum. It is recorded from 1750, for example, that during an inspection of the 1st Dragoon Guards it was noted that trumpeters had been replaced by drummers, which we can take to mean kettledrummers because of the mounted status of this regiment in the British army. Drum horses are traditionally heavy 'Shire-horse-types' which are large and strong enough to be kitted out to carry a pair of kettledrums. They have to be strong because when they are fully ready for parade, drum horses can be loaded down with over 450lbs in weight, and when taking into account the rider-drummer, all the equipment, the saddle and the two drums of either silver or brass, this makes the load equivalent to two men on its back. To put this into some kind of perspective, the weight carried in this role exceeded that carried by horses ridden into battle by fully armoured knights during battles such as Agincourt in 1415. Kettledrum horses are parade ground pieces and are familiar images particularly on the large-scale ceremonial parades and are not expected to move fast, but at a more sedate pace to maintain contact with the marching bands it accompanies. It takes on average around 18 months to train a drum horse and it is just as well that these horses have an inherently docile nature because the drummer uses both hands to play the drums and the only way to control his horse is by using special reins with his legs and feet. The drums have to be well balanced on the animal's back and they are attached by means of special harnesses. Drum horses are still to be found in use within the military, especially the Household Cavalry regiments of the Life Guards and the Blues & Royals, who use them on ceremonial duties, including in Trooping the Colour. The Nazi regime in Germany during the 1930s also used drum horses in a display which was reminiscent of the height of the Prussian army in the nineteenth century. The grand military parades have long since passed into history, leaving us today with tantalising glimpses of what it must have been like when we see the drum horses on parade at ceremonies such as Trooping the Colour.

The drum in military use began its service life as a ceremonial instrument and gradually over time was elevated from its humble tribal origins to become prominent on the battlefields around the world for more than 4,500 years. It has been used as a device for signalling, to maintain morale and to attract recruits to the ranks of the army. The drum has been used for a variety of roles within the military, from improvised table tops to announcing punishments. In its heyday in the eighteenth and nineteenth centuries, the drum stood out from other instruments before finally being consigned to ceremonial parades once again at the start of the twentieth century. Today drums are to be seen on display in military museums around the world, such as the French Musée de l'Empéri in Provence and *Les Invalides* in Paris, where many Regimental Colours of Napoleon's grand battalions are displayed, and the National Army Museum in London. The Royal Gloucestershire, Berkshire and Wiltshire Regiment at the Wardrobe in Salisbury, Wiltshire has various drums on display as regimental souvenirs from campaigns, such as an example of an Afghan drum acquired in 1880 during the Second Afghan War where the 66th Regiment of Foot lost 286 killed and thirty-two wounded at the Battle of Maiwand on 27 July that year. It is rudimentary in style, but still has the same function as military drums and even drums from other regions and cultures around the world. Other drum artefacts at this same museum include a Russian '*naker*-type' drum captured during the Crimean War, which would have been carried on a man's back while a second beat it using two sticks. There is also another smaller Russian drum from the same period and a German drum captured during the First World War, both of which were used on special occasions in the officers' mess.

There are quite literally hundreds of regimental museums all across Europe and the United States of America, and all over Britain. Even Jersey and Guernsey in the Channel Islands have their own separate museums where the regalia of the islands' militia forces can be seen on display. On Jersey the collection of the Royal Jersey Militia is housed at Elizabeth Castle where piles of drums are on display in the same way as the larger museums. Some churches and cathedrals have Regimental Colours 'laid up', which is to say hung in a way so that the flags are suspended to show the battle honours. These buildings, like the museums, make fascinating places to visit; buildings such as St Mary's church in Taunton, Somerset where the Colours of the Somerset Light Infantry hang, or Norwich Cathedral in Norfolk where there are memorials and the Regimental Colours of the Royal Norfolk Regiment. The Regimental Colours of the Dorset Regiment are laid up in Sherborne Abbey, Somerset and to see these is to see the history of the regiment. So, when next visiting one of these museums, take time to give more than just a passing glance at the drums on display, because they have a great deal to tell about the regiment's history. As for the drummers themselves, they are still soldiers first and foremost, and as such they have had to accept the changes in their roles and adapt to rise to the challenges in the same way that soldiers have done throughout the centuries.

BIBLIOGRAPHY

Beckett, Ian F.W., *Discovering English County Regiments*. Shire Publications, Buckinghamshire, 2003.

Brereton, J.M., *The British Soldier: A Social History from 1661 to the Present Day*. Bodley Head Ltd, London, 1986.

Carver, Field Marshal Lord, *The Seven Ages of the British Army*. Grafton Books, London, 1986.

Chandler, David G., *The Art of Warfare on Land*. Hamlyn, London, 1974.

Davis, Brian L., *German Army Uniforms and Insignia 1933–1945*. Lionel Leventhal, London, 1971.

Duncan, John and John Walton, *Heroes for Victoria*. Spellmount, Kent, 1991.

Dyer, Gwynne, *War*. Bodley Head, London, 1985.

Featherstone, Donald, *Weapons & Equipment of the Victorian Soldier*. Arms and Armour Press, London, 1996.

Ffoulkes, Charles, *Arms & Armament*. George G. Harrap & Co., London, 1945.

Grbasic, Z. and V. Vuksic., *The History of the Cavalry*. Copublishing, Switzerland, 1989.

Hamilton, Jill, *Marengo; The Myth of Napoleon's Horse*. Fourth Estate Ltd, London, 2000.

Haswell, Jock, *The British Army; A Concise History*. Thames and Hudson, London, 1975.

Haythornthwaite, Philip, *Weapons & Equipment of the Napoleonic Wars*. Arms & Armour, London, 1998.

Holmes, Richard, *Firing Line*. Jonathan Cape, London, 1985.

Holmes, Richard, *Redcoat*. Harper Collins, London, 2002.

Holmes, Richard, *Sahib; The British Soldier in India*. Harper Collins, London, 2005.

Hook, Jason and Richard, *American Indian Warrior Chiefs*. Firebird Books, Poole, Dorset, 1989.

Joinville & Villehardouin, *Chronicles of the Crusades*. M.R.B. Shaw; Penguin Books Ltd, 1963.

Keegan, John, *The Face of Battle*. Barrie & Jenkins, London, 1988.

Keegan, John, *A History of Warfare*. Pimlico, London, 1994.

Keegan, John and Richard Holmes, *Soldier: A History of Men in Battle*. Sphere Books, London, 1987.

Kerr, Paul, *The Crimean War*. Boxtree, London, 1997.

Lawford, James (ed.), *The Cavalry*. Roxby Press, London, 1976.

MacDonald, Lyn, *1914*. Michael Joseph Ltd, London, 1987.

Mayne, Richard, *The Battle of Jersey*. Phillimore, London, 1981.

Montgomery, *Field Marshal Viscount of Alamein: A History of Warfare*. Collins, London, 1968.

Nicolle, David, *Medieval Warfare Source Book: Volume 1: Warfare in Western Christendom*. Arms and Armour Press, London, 1995.

Nicolle, David, *Medieval Warfare Source Book: Christian Europe and its Neighbours*. Arms and Armour Press, London, 1996.

Pivka, Otto von, *Armies of the Napoleonic Era*. David & Charles, Newton Abbot, Devon, 1979.

Richardson, Robert, *Larrey; Surgeon to Napoleon's Imperial Guard*. Quiller Press, London, 1974.

Rothenberg, Gunther, *The Napoleonic Wars*. Cassell, London, 2001.

Rothenberg, Gunther, *The Art of Warfare in the Age of Napoleon*. Spellmount, Kent, 1997.

Urban, Mark, *Fusiliers*. Faber & Faber Ltd., London, 2007.

Vuksic, V., and Z. Grbasic, *Cavalry: The History of a Fighting Elite*, Cassell, London, 1993.

Woolrych, Austin, *Battles of the English Civil War*. Pimlico, London, 1991.

Wykes, Alan, *Nuremberg Rallies*. MacDonal and Co. Ltd, London, 1969.

INDEX